John

MW00761944

Dark Night Experience

Survive, Revive and Thrive

outskirtspress
DENVER, COLORADO

The opinions expressed in this manuscript are solely the opinions of the author and do not represent the opinions or thoughts of the publisher. The author has represented and warranted full ownership and/or legal right to publish all the materials in this book.

Dark Night Experience
Survive, Revive and Thrive
All Rights Reserved.
Copyright © 2015 John and Vivian Moy
v4.0

Cover Photo © 2015 thinkstockphotos.com All rights reserved - used with permission.

All Scripture quotations, unless otherwise indicated, are taken from the Holy Bible, NEW INTERNATIONAL VERSION. Copyright (C) 1973, 1978, 1984 by International Bible Society. Used by permission of Zondervan Bible Publishers.

This book may not be reproduced, transmitted, or stored in whole or in part by any means, including graphic, electronic, or mechanical without the express written consent of the publisher except in the case of brief quotations embodied in critical articles and reviews.

Outskirts Press, Inc.
http://www.outskirtspress.com

ISBN: 978-1-4787-4467-2

Library of Congress Control Number: 2014921274

Outskirts Press and the "OP" logo are trademarks belonging to Outskirts Press, Inc.

PRINTED IN THE UNITED STATES OF AMERICA

Contents

Part II: Thrive with the GPS CROWN Gifts

Dedication in Remembrance of Helen Ling (29 March 1916 - 6 February 2013)

Helen was Vivian's beloved mother and my mother-in-law for over 40 years. Her testimony is in chapter 18, entitled "The Wounded Healer."

In all the years that I knew Helen, I have not met a more beloved and blessed woman. She walked through many Dark Night experiences with the Lord. Helen embodied the reality of her life and faith in the Lord Jesus Christ and the truths written in this book.

She touched many lives that, in turn, touched thousands of others. Her 96 years of life testify to the faithfulness and trustworthiness of our Savior in the midst of devastating losses, agonizing loneliness, and deprivation. Through wars and displacements, widowhood and singleness, sicknesses and challenges, the God she knew and served never once failed her as she single-handedly sought to raise two young daughters to adulthood. She was well acquainted with grief and knew intimately the amazing gifts and the grace of God described in this book.

Helen was ushered into her heavenly home on February 6, 2013. This book is dedicated to the memory of her as one whose life demonstrates, "that in all things God works for the good of those who love him, who have been called according to his purpose" (Rom 8:28).

She was truly the wounded healer who was **"sorrowful, yet always rejoicing; poor, yet making many rich; having nothing, and yet possessing everything" (2 Cor 6:10).**

With love

To

Olivia

with

Ethan

&

Dylan

Esther & Mike

Deborah & Joe

"What we have heard and known

We will tell the next generation

The praiseworthy deeds of the Lord,

His power, and the wonders he has done.

So the next generation would know them,

Even the children yet to be born,

And they in turn would tell their children.

Then they would put their trust in God

And would not forget his deeds

But would keep his commands."

Psalm 78:3-7

Introduction: Four Shocking Discoveries of the Dark Night Experience

The Chinese have a saying, "Every family has its painful secrets." People say that there are two certainties in life: death and taxes. Well, they missed one: the Dark Night Experience (DNX).

What is the Dark Night Experience (DNX)? Dark Night Experiences are those awful, painful, and terrible experiences in life that shock the core of our being and fill us with anguish, bewilderment, helplessness, and hopelessness.

An ugly divorce. Sudden death of a loved one. Suicide. Betrayal. Cancer. Addiction. Chronic pain. Bankruptcy. Violent crime. Abandonement. Accidents. Long term disability. Job loss. Natural disasters. Singleness. Childlessness. Heavy debts. War. Family conflicts and strife. Persecution.

It is like living through a tsunami and having every aspect of your life marked with a giant X that says "shattered, condemned, and marked for destruction."

Someone once described to me his DNX: "I was like a wounded insect crawling around in circles, leaving behind a trail of blood and guts." In my third DNX I was crawling around in pain and turmoil with tormenting questions that had no answers. So I started to take notes, ask questions, and do research on the DNX. Then, I discovered four **shocking realities** of this awful DNX. **First**, I discovered that everyone, I mean everyone, goes through this darkness at some time in life. Some go through it more than once. I was surprised to learn that the highest suicide rate in the US is associated with those age 45 to 64[1], at a stage in life which many consider to be the most productive, where individuals "have arrived." Somehow, their past experiences, know-how, and achievements fail to prepare them for the unexpected and shattering events later in life.

In my desperate search for understanding and answers, I was not able to find any resources that could identify the tormenting questions which I could not put into words. I longed to read the experiences of others on the Dark Night. But the books I found were too lengthy and detailed for my desperate heart and depleted energy to plow through. So for this book, I purposely include many short but raw, first-hand DNX stories that I hope will enlighten, encourage, instruct, and inspire all of us. **(I have left out names and changed certain details of the stories in order to protect the privacy of the individuals involved. Sources of stories in direct quotes are in the footnotes.)**

Second, I discovered that we humans are hardwired to ask tormenting questions in our DNX. Many of us will try to

---

1   "Fashion Designer L'Wren Scott Found Dead in Apparent Suicide in NYC." Narr. Diane Sawyer *ABC World News*. ABC. 17 Mar 2014. http://abcnews.go.com/Entertainment/fashion-designer-lwren-scott-found-dead-apparent-suicide/story?id=22942050

"numb and dumb" the pains of our tormenting questions with destructive behaviors. In the movie *Wyatt Earp*, the main character, Wyatt, allowed his tormenting grief to poison his life. Until the unexpected death of his bride Wyatt was a fine and hardworking young man. To cope with his grief, Wyatt got drunk and made a series of bad choices that landed him in jail, charged with the hanging offense of stealing a horse. During a visit across the prison bars, Wyatt's father appealed to his son, "Life is all about losses. Just because you lost your wife, it does not give you the excuse to destroy your life."

Third, I discovered that most of us do not know how to survive, revive, and thrive in DNX. This book provides a two part strategy. First, I identify and answer ten tormenting questions and griefs of the DNX; second, I introduce eight gifts from God that enable us to walk through this deep darkness.

What is grief? It is a gaping hole in our hearts resulting from losses. The greater the loss, the deeper the grief and the bigger the hole is. Grief reminds us of losses of the past, the present, and the potential future. Grief is universal, but the journey through grief in DNX is unique and personal with its own timetable. We may try to bury our grief but we can never outrun it. Grief goes wherever we go. Grief usually, though not always, comes with grievances toward someone and/or something. When we accuse others of causing our grief we end up living with anger and bitterness. When we curse ourselves for the loss we experience crippling guilt, anxiety, fear, and stress that compound the heavy burdens we already carry.

Why is it so hard to deal with grief? Because it is like one soldier said, "I can feel the itch of my amputated arm but

I cannot scratch it." In our grief we are confronted by **four deep-seated, crippling fears** that paralyze us:

1. **Make it**—all of us wonder if we are going to make it through the horrible darkness and have a decent future. I once asked a dear friend who was going through a bitter divorce, "What is foremost on your mind these days?" He answered without hesitation, "I am worrying about my finances, my loneliness, my retirement, and my children's future."

2. **Make sense**—"I don't understand. It does not make sense to me." This fear and anguish of trying to understand an experience like the Dark Night proves to be more intense for those who know the love of God in Christ. Kierkegaard wrote, "Life can only be understood backwards; but it must be lived forwards." The problem is that we want to know now and not later.

Will we ever make sense of what happened to us? I remember a movie scene of two policemen driving by a rocky hill overlooking a town on a reserve. The rock faces were tagged with big, bold, multi-colored graffiti. "The graffiti looks like ugly blots that make no sense," the younger policeman wondered out loud. In reply, the older policeman said, "When you are in the right place, looking at it from the right direction, you will know the message." Sure enough, when they later stood on the back porch of a young lady's house, they read the message that said, "I love you." It is our hope that this book will position you in the right place with the right perspective to start making sense of your DNX.

3. **Make it right**—we all have an innate sense for justice and mercy. We want to see wrongs "made right." We want pay back for those who are complicit in our DNX while we demand a second, third, and fourth chance for ourselves. Will what happened to us in our DNX ever be made right?

4. **Make a difference**—there is a fear deep down in our soul of being stuck in a "shattered, condemned, and marked for destruction" life sentence. We lament how our life in DNX is so unfair, unjust, unwanted, and wasteful. We wonder if any good could ever come out of it. We need to know that our pain has not been "wasted" but is "worth it." Substantial healing will eventually come when we realize in our personal experience that our DNX has made a positive difference in our lives and in others. Teaching, sharing, and writing this book has been part of the "make it," "make sense," "make it right," and "make a difference" journey for me.

Fourth, I discovered that in our DNX God is not rocking our boat, but sinking our boat. In our DNX we are like people in a shipwreck. After barely surviving, we find ourselves landed on foreign soil with a foreign culture and language and nothing more than the tattered clothes on our backs. If we are to survive on land we have to be willing to learn a whole new way of living and relating. Previous experiences and expectations no longer fit. We cannot afford to stubbornly hold on to life as we used to know it. We have to learn not to look backward and demand our old boat and life, but to change by taking small, baby "faith-walk" steps forward.

Winston Churchill declared during WWII that our darkest hour can be our finest hour. May you in your DNX also find your finest hour in discovering "the treasures of darkness, riches stored in secret places" (Is 45:3).

Chuck Colson was one of the closest confidants of President Nixon. He went to jail for being part of the Watergate scandal. His new life in Christ touched thousands upon thousands of inmates and others around the world. Here is the **testimony of Charles Colson on his Dark Night Experience.**

"I am a product of the best in evangelicalism: converted 32 years ago in a flood of tears after hearing the gospel, discipled by a strong prayer group, taught by great theologians. ... What happens in the dark night of the soul? I found out this past year. Weeks after finishing *The Good Life*, my son Wendell was diagnosed with bone cancer. The operation to remove a malignant tumor took 10 hours—the longest day of my life. Wendell survived, but he's still in chemo.

"I had barely caught my breath when my daughter, Emily, was diagnosed with melanoma. Back in the hospital, I again prayed fervently. Soon after, my wife, Patty, underwent major knee surgery. Where was my good life? Exhausted from hospitals, two years of writing The Good Life, and an ugly situation with a disgruntled former employee, I found myself wrestling with the Prince of Darkness, who attacks us when we are weakest. I walked around at night, asking God why he would allow this. Alone, shaken, fearful, I longed for the closeness with God I had experienced even in the darkest days of prison.

"An answer came in September. I was standing alone on the deck of a friend's home in North Carolina, overlooking the spectacular Smoky Mountains arising out of the mist. I was moved

> *What happens when you have relied on intimacy with God, and the day comes when he seems distant?*

by the glory of God's creation. It's impossible not to know God as the Creator, I realized, for there is no other rational explanation for reality. God cannot not be. It struck me that I don't have to make sense of the agonies I bear or hear a clear answer. God is not a creature of my emotions or senses. God is God, the one who created me and takes responsibility for my children's destiny and mine. I can only cling to the certainty that he is and he has spoken.... 'When thy God hides his face, say not that he has forgotten thee,' Spurgeon once wrote. 'He is but tarrying a little while to make thee love him better, and when he cometh, thou shalt have joy in the Lord and shalt rejoice with joy unspeakable.'

"Following the events of 2005, my faith deepened. Countless times over the years I've experienced God and his providence, but I've also known the dark night. God, I've realized, is not just the friend who takes my hand, but also the great, majestic Creator who reigns forever."[2]

How to get the most out of this book?

This book is written with many interesting stories and quotes to explain and illustrate the life-changing truth of God. Some of you may find it helpful to look at the table of contents and

2 Charles Colson with Anne Morse, "My Soul's Dark Night." *Christianity Today*. December 2005, Vol. 49, No. 12, P. 80. www.christianitytoday.com/ct/2005/december/15.80.html

read first those chapters on topics relevant to you at this time of your life. If you read this book straight through, I encourage you to take time to read it slowly and prayerfully, with breaks to digest and nourish your soul. For those who are in the Dark Night Experience, do take time and effort to do the action steps at the end of each chapter. No matter which way you choose to approach the book, I pray that your vision of God will be enlarged, your faith in God strengthened, your life enriched, and your influence in the world increasingly impactful.

Actions (for personal and group study):

1. What have you learned about the DNX from this introduction? Write in a notebook your Dark Night Experience.

2. What is grief? Why is it so hard to deal with grief?

3. In what way does Colson's testimony add to your understanding of yourself, God, and the DNX?

4. Bring your questions, doubts, and concerns to God in prayer and start reading the gospel of John in the Bible.

Part I
Survive and Revive Through
the Ten Tormenting Griefs

CHAPTER 1

The Grief of Being Shattered

Zig Ziglar said, "There is no grief that I have experienced that has come close to my grief over the loss of our child. Throughout our months and years of grieving, faith has been the redeeming force that has enabled us to bear the pain and continue to live in victory. The very process of grief is given to us by a loving, heavenly Father. God uses grief to heal us, strengthen us in our faith, and cause us to grow in our relationship with Him."[3]

Suddenly, the ominous clouds that we have dreaded and denied burst and our lives are shattered like a broken glass vase on a hardwood floor. We find ourselves stuck in GAS (**g**uilt, **g**rief, **a**nger, **a**nxiety, **s**nare, **s**hackle, and **s**hame), which consumes our every waking thought and invades our sleepless nights.

"At the age of 30 I never dreamed that I would be divorced with two young children," a young mother lamented. After a few years

---

3   Robert H. Schuller. *Turning Hurts into Halos and Scars into Stars* (Nashville: Thomas Nelson Inc., 1999) 210.

of painful struggles she was able to admit, "I am finally picking up the pieces of my life." "Great!" I said, "God is able to glue them back together then." "Not quite," she replied, "God won't be doing that. He will have to melt and mold the pieces into something new." What an insight into the DNX! God does not want us to be a glued together, broken vessel with glaring scars and wounds for all to see or for us to hide. Instead, God wants to make us whole, beautiful, and useful again. Even though the restoring process of melting and molding may be gut-wrenching, painful, and tedious, it has great long-term rewards.

John and Vivian: "Over 25 years ago, my wife and I experienced what we thought was our first DNX. In our agony we could not even pray but just knelt and groaned by our bed. Then I read these surprising words by Teresa of Avila, 'God took my dreams, ground them into powder, and then blew them away… I don't even treat my dog the way God treated me.' I exclaimed loudly in agreement, 'Yes-s-s! Finally someone understood how I was feeling.'"

As I look back on my 69 years of life, I realize my DNXs were God's way of setting me free from my many childhood wounds. I remember one painful episode in Hong Kong when I was around 10 years old. I overheard a neighbor telling someone about me, "He is a child without a mother." I was shocked by what I heard. I remember thinking, "That's not true!! I *have* a mother. I just don't know where she is at the moment. But I *do* have a mother." Even though I was reunited with my mother a few years later, I still grew up into an angry, rebellious, and hurting young adult with everything bottled up inside me. I was like 'dynamite looking for a match.' Whenever I found a match, it always blew up in my face.

After I became a Christian I somehow expected the blessed life in Christ would be the easy life of peace and plenty, happiness and no hassles. Then I heard a testimony of someone who grew up in the South and lived in Los Angeles as an engineer. God called him back to the South to serve his people with the Gospel through meeting social needs. He was beaten and left for dead, suffered deprivation and mistreatment, but witnessed healthy growth in the community and people becoming followers of Christ. He said something very strange and radical to me, "The easy life is not the good life."

The question, then, is **what is the truly blessed life?** Genesis 35:23-26; 37; 39-50

As one of the 12 sons of Jacob, Joseph was an immature and spoiled boy at the age of 17. Jacob, in his old age, contributed to the hatred between Joseph and his brothers by openly flaunting his affection for Joseph and showering him with gifts, like the richly-ornamented robe. He even had Joseph report on his older brothers' activities. Furthermore, God gave Joseph two dreams that further inflamed the sibling rivalry, which resulted in the brothers selling Joseph into slavery in Egypt for the sum of 20 days' wages. In an instant, Joseph's privileged life came to an abrupt end. From being his father's favorite son, Joseph's life was now "shattered, condemned, and marked for destruction and slavery." Joseph did not ask for what happened to him. God also did not ask Joseph's permission to put him through the ringer. Joseph, in his DNX, went through all 10 tormenting griefs and questions written in this book, exhibiting for us what a blessed and successful life truly is.

Why didn't God prevent Joseph from being sold as a slave?

After Joseph became the second in command under Pharaoh in Egypt two sons were born to him. He "named the first born Manasseh, and said, 'It is because God has made me forget all my trouble and all my father's household.' The second son he named Ephraim and said, 'It is because God has made me fruitful in the land of my suffering.'" (Gn 41:51-52). In Joseph's healing process, God made him **forget** and become **fruitful** as Joseph faced the four deep-seated fears of his DNX:

1. "Can I *make it* through?"—Scriptures repeatedly tells us that "the Lord was with Joseph," enabling him to make it through all his years of slavery and afflictions (Gn 49:2).

2. "Can I *make* things *right?*"—God enabled Joseph to make things right with his brothers. "Then Joseph said to his brothers, 'Come close to me.' When they had done so, he said, 'I am your brother, Joseph, the one you sold into Egypt!'" (Gn 45:4). Joseph further reassured his brothers, "Don't be afraid. I will provide for you and your children" (Gn 50:21).

3. "Can I *make sense* of what happened?"—As God helped Joseph make sense of his suffering and pain, Joseph was able to comfort his brothers in saying, "And now, do not be distressed and do not be angry with yourselves for selling me here, because it was to save lives that God sent me ahead of you" (Gn 45:5).

4. "Can I *make a positive difference?*"—Joseph testified to his positive contribution in the wise counsel and purpose of God for his family. "For two years now

there has been famine in the land, and for the next five years there will not be plowing and reaping. But God sent me ahead of you to preserve for you a remnant on earth and to save your lives by a great deliverance" (Gn 45:6-7).

After 13 years of slavery and nine years of fruitfulness, Joseph finally came to understand why God did not prevent "bad" things from happening to him. God's answer to human injustice and sufferings is the making of a person to be His saving agent of change. As Joseph chose to walk in God's presence (Gn 39:2, 3, 21-23), he saw firsthand God's purpose for his suffering in saving many lives (Gn 50:20). This purpose involves the sovereign and arduous process of transforming Joseph from an immature and inexperienced boy of 17 into an influential and inspiring leader through his DNX.

What lessons then can we learn from Joseph's DNX?

- No matter what happens to us, God promises us His presence, provision, and power right now.

- Why didn't God prevent what happened to Joseph? Because God had a God-sized purpose to help Joseph grow up and become God's instrument to bless His people.

- Joseph chose to walk with God in his DNX and witnessed the fulfillment of His purpose.

- Just like with Joseph in his DNX, God will also sovereignly weave together our talents, giftedness, personality, culture, experience, weaknesses, and strengths to glorify Him and fulfill His plans.

- What brings glory to God is always the best for us in the long run, but involves us trusting and obeying Him in good times and tough times.

- Joseph demonstrated to us that a life truly blessed by God is a life lived in trust and obedience to God, regardless of the circumstances we are in. If God is able to make Joseph forget and become fruitful even in and through his DNX, God is able to do the same in us if we resolve to trust and obey Him.

On this journey through the Dark Night, all of us will be tempted to take short cuts. But God has provided a way of escape as well as the grace of forgiveness when we mess up. According to 1 Corinthians 10:13, "No temptation has seized you except what is common to man. And God is faithful; he will not let you be tempted beyond what you can bear. But when you are tempted, he will also provide a way out so that you can stand up under it." As I reflected on the occasions when I sinned, I realized that God did leave me prior warnings, as well as a way of escape. It was my stubborn and willful choices that got me into deeper and deeper troubles.

Lesson from a branch—I remember a lady missionary who spoke at our church. She had a knife in one hand and a leafy branch in the other hand. As she started to talk she began to cut away the leaves and the bark. When we finally realized that she was making an arrow from the branch we began to understand the stripping away process in DNX. A word picture from Isaiah 49:2 came to mind, **"He made me into a polished arrow and concealed me in his quiver."** We know that it is impossible to shoot accurately at a target with an arrow encumbered with flowers and leaves. Our accomplishments, sense of security and significance, reputation, etc., are like the beautiful flowers and lush green leaves that God whittles away in our DNX.

How many of us misunderstand God as being cruel and wasteful as we watch the petals and leaves being ripped from the branches of our lives? We complain. We accuse God of being unfair, unloving, and uncaring. We are convinced that God did not know what He was doing, or maybe we think that God is powerless to stop the humiliating process. Meanwhile, God keeps on pressing ahead silently to make the finished product—a polished arrow.

After stripping, there is the sanding, cutting, and repeated polishing, and lastly, the splitting of the ends, one for the feathers and one for the tip. These are all very painful steps for us to endure. At least it is finished now, right? Ready to be used? Not quite! The last part of Isaiah 49:2 tells us that God then conceals us, the beautiful polished arrow, in the dark place of his quiver.

Really! We impatiently ask, "How long do we have to stay in the dark?" The Father's answer is, "Humble yourselves, therefore, under God's mighty hand, that he may lift you up in due time. Cast all your anxiety on him because he cares for you" (1Pt 5:6-7). *Humbling* means to bow and submit to God's will and timing, to be under the mighty, wise, and purposeful hand of God. God promised He would move at His perfect time, and not our "due time." The polished arrows will stay in His quiver until the right moment for the right target.

So, be patient. Rest in your loving Father's quiver! He knows what He is doing.

Actions (for personal and group study):

1. What have you gleaned from reading Joseph's story about God, yourself, and life?

2. What are the questions the branch-to-arrow illustration answers, and what are the questions and concerns this illustration creates?

3. "An unexamined life is not worth living." (Socrates) Is this statement true? Why or why not?

4. Memorize and reflect on the three assurances of God to each of us in Jeremiah 29:11, "'For I know the plans I have for you,' declared the Lord, 'plans to prosper you and not to harm you, plans to give you hope and a future.'"

5. Continue reading the gospel of John and tell God in prayer about your struggles, concerns, and what He is teaching you at this time of your life.

CHAPTER 2

The Grief of Tormenting Questions

In the midst of her DNX, Robin Norwood, author and new age counselor for alcohol addiction wrote, "Why *ME?* Why *this?* Why *now?* Who among us hasn't been driven in times of trouble to demand answers to these questions? We search our hearts. We query life. We rail at God. We rant at any sympathetic listener. *Why?* And the replies that come back—vague, general palliatives that cannot begin to address our particular pain and frustration—feel empty, impersonal, even maddening.

"'Time heals all things.'

'You're upset now, but you'll get over it.'

"'It's God's will and not for us to question.'

"'It's Fate.'

"'These things just happen.'

"Perhaps the most impossible bit of advice when we're over-whelmed by our difficulty is 'Try not to dwell on it. Thinking about it will only make you feel worse.' Words offered by well-meaning friends, helpless in the face of our distress, leave us shipwrecked and unsoothed on the shoals of what-ever has gone so very, very wrong. We drag ourselves wearily over the bruising details of our lives until eventually we find that time does indeed heal much after all, though sorrow and suffering have left deep and indelible tracks across the heart...

"I was divorcing my husband; no longer working as a therapist ... I was seriously ill and slowly dying... The following morn-ing as I was wheeled into surgery... [,] with deep disappoint-ment in myself and my life, I slipped under the anesthetic." [4]

Edith Schaffer wrote, "Do people swarm around you when you have gone through a tragedy of some sort and nearly destroy you with the kind of 'comfort' which Job's comfort-ers threw at him? 'There must be something wrong with your prayer life.' Or, 'God must be pointing to a terrible sin in your life. You'd better search your heart.' Or, 'I'm sure that if you had more faith your child would be healed.' Or, 'I know it will all turn out right. If you let Jesus lead you, you won't have difficulties like this anymore.' Or, 'What you need is a real "experience," then you won't have any more problems; every day will be filled with perfect joy.' Every sentence of such 'comfort' comes out as a criticism and a comparison." [5]

"A loving silence often has far more power to heal and to

---

4   Robin Norwood. *Why Me. Why This. Why Now: A Guide to Answering Life's Toughest Questions* (Toronto: McClelland & Stewart Inc., 1994), 1-4.
5   Edith Schaeffer. *Affliction* (Old Tappan: Fleming H. Revell Company, 1978), p31

connect than the most well-intentioned words,"[6] wrote Rachel Naomi Remen.

My naïve doubting says, "What happens if God cannot answer my tormenting questions? Will these questions destroy my faith?" The reality is that there has never been a question that God or others have not asked and answered. Many honest seekers have asked challenging questions that eventually led them to find true wisdom and God. So go ahead and ask, seek, knock, and find!

What are the tormenting questions all of us ask in our DNX?

Winston Churchill once said, "There are two things you do not ask, 'how a decision was made and what is in the sausage.'" However, when our lives are "shattered, condemned, and marked for destruction," we are hardwired to ask questions that torment. These question marks are like fishing hooks (???) that twist our hearts in painful turmoil. They must be taken out firmly but gently by God, at His timing, when we are ready.

Gideon did not have to rehearse his angry, tormenting questions because he had been asking them for seven years. He was furious with God because of the repeated setbacks and failures he witnessed in his own life and in the land due to God's silence and lack of action. For seven years, the Midianites ravaged God's people (Jgs 6). When Gideon finally came face to face with God, he swung at God with double jabs and a knockout punch. Gideon did what many of us are tempted to do when God is mentioned in any conversation in

---

6   www.wisdomquotes.com/quote/rachel-naomi-remen.html

our DNX. We want to vent our rage by tearing a strip off of someone or anyone, especially those closest to us.

Surprisingly, God is not offended when we openly speak our mind. Gideon survived his savage attack on the Almighty without being turned into a rack of burnt Chinese BBQ spare-ribs. God also did not apologize for not answering Gideon for seven years, nor did He back down from Gideon's misguided attacks. I believe the reason is because no answer would satisfy Gideon in the midst of his emotional turmoil. It is the same way with us today. God would rather suffer our accusation and blame for a season as He continues to patiently demonstrate His timely, wise, gracious, and gentle care for us until our hearts are ready to hear from Him.

Gideon's first jab : the tormenting "if" question

Gideon's first jab was the wearisome "if" question, "**[I]f the Lord is with us …**" (Jgs 6:13).

If I did or did not …**If** God did or did not …. **If** he or she did or did not …**If** I knew …**If** it did or did not ….**What if** …? **Only if** …**If** … **If**.

How many of us have been tormented by these two loaded letters? No matter how hard we try, we cannot seem to get away from them. Many spend an insane amount of time doing postmortems on past happenings, hoping to change the outcome. We frantically try to change the unchangeable without success. Gideon was angry because God let bad things happen to His people; God should have intervened but God did not.

Gideon demanded answers from God, but God did not give him the satisfaction of a reply. It really infuriates us when God is silent and does not answer our questions according to our timetable, which is right here and right now. So we conclude that our God must not be real, that He is powerless to do anything, or that maybe He does not care.

Gideon's second jab : the torturous 3 *Ws*

Gideon's first jab did not seem to affect God, so he unleashed a second set of jabs. It is the infamous three-part question that all humankind asks in our pain and doubt. "[I]f the LORD is with us, **why** has all this happened to us? **Where** are all his wonders that our fathers told us about **when** they said, 'Did not the LORD bring us up out of Egypt?'" (Jgs 6:13a).

These torturous questions scream of lament, pain, and protest. From the depth of his grieving heart Gideon cried out, in Joyce Meyers's words, "Why God, why, when God, when, and where God, where?" This three-fold question can be framed in many other ways. "God, **why** did you or didn't you do this?" "God, **where** were you when I needed you?" "**Where** is the justice in all that is happening?" "God, **when** are you going to vindicate me and answer my prayers like you used to?" "**When** are you going to punish those who did wrong?"

What was God's response to Gideon's tormenting questions? The purpose of jabs in boxing is to weaken the opponent. God took Gideon's jabs but did not weaken His resolve to stay SILENT FOR SEVEN YEARS!

Gideon's KO (knockout) punch

Gideon did not get any satisfaction from his jabs at God. Then Gideon unleashed his deadly knockout punch, saying, "But now the Lord has abandoned us and put us into the hand of Midian" (Jgs 6:13b).

Gideon concluded that God was the culprit of all his and his people's trouble. I can just see Gideon's anger intensifying as he swung at God verbally. He was pumping his fist toward the heavens and spitting out louder and angrier accusations, "God, you are responsible for all the evil that is happening to us. You abandoned us and did not help us. God you should have …. I would have ….You put us in harm's way by putting us into the hands of the Midianites."

Like many of us, Gideon forgot why the Israelites were in their sad condition. It was not God, but their own choice to do "evil in the eyes of the LORD" (Jgs 6:1) and "what was right in their own eyes" (Jgs 21:25, ESV) that resulted in their bondage and sufferings.

Four revealing discoveries from Gideon's encounter with God in Judges 6

1. The simmering, tormenting questions are like hooks that pierce deeply into our souls.

2. Surprisingly, God never responds directly to Gideon's accusations. The eternal God has no need to defend His actions or seeming inactions. Once in a while, God may surprise us by giving us glimpses of an

answer that makes sense to us. A few particularly thorny questions may even disappear with the passing of time. Along the way we gain the confidence that God knows what He is doing and not doing. One day, when we see God face to face, He will answer all our questions to our full satisfaction. At that time, no one, not even one, can or will find fault or associate any evil or malice with God.

3. God did not find fault in Gideon, who protested honestly and truthfully. James 1:5 says, "If any of you lacks wisdom, he should ask God, who gives generously to all *without finding fault*, and it will be given to him." God genuinely values our coming to Him and asking Him for wisdom. He loves and cares for us more deeply than we could ever imagine.

4. Even though God was silent in answering Gideon's outburst, He did address five critical questions that Gideon did not know enough to ask but that prove to be relevant even for us today:

Who are you, God? "The LORD is with you." (Jgs 6:12).

Who am I? God called Gideon "a mighty warrior" (Jgs 6:12). What a curious perspective of someone who was "beating out wheat in the winepress to hide it from the Midianites." Only God can see us as more than what meets the eye. He does not see us as we are, but as what we can be in Him, a mighty warrior. God continues to encourage and inspire us to live up to His vision for us.

Do you really love and care for me? God's commitment to Gideon, as it is to us, is in the promise, "The Lord is with you." His presence is His stamp of love and approval of us.

God, what do you want me to do now? "The LORD ... said, 'Go in the strength you have and save Israel out of Midian's hand. Am I not sending you?' 'But, Lord,' Gideon asked, 'how can I save Israel? My clan is the weakest in Manasseh, and I am the least in my family.' The LORD answered, 'I will be with you, and you will strike down all the Midianites together'" (Jgs 6:14-16). *God has a plan.* He gives each of us a strategic and vital part in negotiating and carrying out His plans in and through our Dark Night.

When God, when? It took Gideon seven years to come to this point of encounter with God. God can change you instantly or gradually as you respond to Him in faith and obedience as a child of God.

Actions (for personal and group study):

1. Can you relate to the first two testimonies in this chapter and why?

2. Write down your reflection on Gideon's tormenting questions. What are your tormenting questions? Crystallize and record them in the notebook.

3. Continue reading the gospel of John. Ask God, "If you are truly God, please reveal yourself to me. Please show me your love and care for me."

4. Memorize and reflect on Isaiah 41:10, "So do not fear, for I am with you; do not be dismayed, for I am your God. I will strengthen you and help you; I will uphold you with my righteous right hand." The word *dismay* means anxiously looking about you. These promises are for those who are fearful and anxiously wondering, "What am I going to do? Should I do this or that?"

CHAPTER 3

The Grief of Recurring and Lengthy Struggles

During a graduation weekend, I met a couple whose teenage child died of a sudden illness over 10 years ago. Their grief was still very evident. The husband used the word *jealousy* to describe his pain. I asked him what he meant by that. He said he became jealous when he saw people celebrating their children's graduations, marriages, and birth of grandchildren, and was reminded of his own lost opportunities to experience the same pride and joy others felt.

Suffering and grief are a part of the human experience. To give shape and vision to our own DNX, I would like to share with you what others have to say about the experience.

The following quotes are from the book *Spirituality, Suffering, and Illness* by Lorraine Wright:

- "Suffering completely fills the human soul and con-scious mind, no matter if the suffering is great or lit-tle."—Victor Frankl, Holocaust survivor (35)

- "Suffering [has] many faces" (10)

- "Suffering is raw, personal, and deep. ... Suffering can mean to experience, undergo, or tolerate anguish, grief, loss, and/or unwanted or unanticipated change." (37)

- "Serious illness is a wakeup call about life." (38)

- "Each human being suffers in a way no other human being suffers ... in the final analysis, your pain and my pain are so deeply personal that comparing them can bring scarcely any consolation or comfort."—Henri J.M. Nouwen[7] (47)

- "Suffering does not affect just the person experiencing an illness. Illness is a family affair, and all family members suffer." (48)

Testimony of Irene Gifford, a Christian psychologist

"Paul and I were richly blessed ... Our three children were a joy, passing with hardly a ripple through adolescence into young adulthood ... one in college, one in seminary, and one married and living less than a mile away.

"A big part of my own inner rhythm was based on the love and support of this wonderfully caring man. ... He was never sick, always strong. And then, my world upended.

"First, the diagnosis: Paul had a serious heart ailment. He went into an unusual depression. A month later, Paul shot himself,

7   See Neuwen's testimony in the next chapter.

and my life was torn apart. Compounding the shock and grief, his ashes were stolen in a church burglary.

"Even while being loved and reassured by family, neighbors, and my extended parish family, I tortured myself with guilt. Why had I gone to church that morning when Paul hadn't felt up to it? I was a psychologist—why hadn't I been aware that he was suicidal? I hadn't even been able to help my own husband.

"After a time, however, my agonizing guilt gave way to anger at God. How had He let this happen? Why? Paul didn't deserve the illness, or the depression. My children didn't deserve to lose their father, nor I my husband. What kind of a 'heavenly Father' would treat His children so cruelly?

"We'd prayed so earnestly together for his healing. Our family and friends—even friends of friends from all over the world—had prayed, too. But God had not touched my husband. He had not worked through the doctors. I learned that even the medication had been wrong. *Everything* had gone wrong.

"Even while I was being nourished and upheld by God in my grief, I wrestled with Him. The pain seemed too great to bear. I prayed less, because God seemed indifferent to me. During the struggle that ensued I wrote the poem about Martha ... Searching the Scriptures, I realized that Martha was not my only companion in this keen sorrow, pain, disappointment, and *perhaps even anger* at God. There were others…

"But looking in the Bible, I found, was only the beginning of my journey back to the side of God. It also required long, prayerful looks inside myself at the rift that I had allowed to come between God and me. After a long way, after a long time, I once again began to sense the presence of Christ at my side—to understand (as only He can help *anyone* understand) that He never had been far from me, never had been against me, though I'd accused Him of that and more.

"It was only after much inner work and finding the right path to healing for my inner ache that God's promise through Isaiah became *real* to me: "'For a brief moment … I hid my face from you, but with everlasting kindness I will have compassion on you,' says the Lord, your Redeemer" (Is 54:8). Only by undertaking the inner journey—beyond denial, then beyond anger—can anyone begin to close the rift with God." [8]

Word pictures for DNX

At my first encounter with Christian workers in their DNX 30 years ago, I asked the Lord for a special word for them. God gave me Psalm 66:10-12, **"For you, O God, tested us; you refined us like silver. You brought us into prison and laid burdens on our backs. You let men ride over our heads; we went through fire and water, but you brought us to a place of abundance."**

The word *test* (bahan) and its derivatives occur 32 times in the Old Testament. "[I]t denotes examining to determine essential qualities and integrity. [P]art of the privilege of being God's people is that of being tested. (Jer. 20:12; Ps 11:5; 139:23)."[9]

---

8   William Backus, *Hidden Rift with God* (Minneapolis: Bethany House Publishers, 1990), 11-13.

9   R. Laird Harris, Gleason L. Archer, and Bruce K. Waltke, eds. *Theological Wordbook of the Old Testament,* Vol. I Chicago: Moody Press, 1980), 100.

Seven word pictures to describe this extreme testing in DNX:

1. **The refining of silver:** the painful/fiery trial

   Gold and silver need extreme heat to bring out the dross and the metal's true value. The impurities are so imbedded in the ore that they require multiple periods of intense heat to release them. The refining fire is personally attended by the gold/silversmith who keeps it at just the right temperature for a pre-scribed length of time so that the ore will not be ru-ined. At the right moment, impurities are removed with the greatest of care to preserve the precious metal.

   The fire/heat is likened to the suffering in a fiery tri-al that is deeply painful, unrelenting, and unique-ly personal. It is a painful but comforting picture of how God refines us with the greatest of care for the purpose of adding great value to our lives. As I look down at my wedding band of 42 years, I see a skillfully crafted gold band etched with vines and branches. I am so glad that I am not wearing twenty pounds of gold ore instead.

2. **A bird caught in a trap:** a snare or a prison

   DNX is strangely described here as a bird caught in a snare. It is a picture of imprisonment and con-finement without the possibility of getting free. The future looks blighted and the present dim and grim. We feel like prisoners on death row. There are many different kinds of prisons in which people find themselves. Some are locked up in their own pain and guilt; others are snared in their bitterness and unforgiveness.

Many are mired in regrets and despair. Their hopelessness is why Jesus came to earth to set humanity free. In Luke 4:18-19, Jesus proclaimed His mission, "The Spirit of the Lord is on me, because he has anointed me *to preach good news to the poor. He has sent me to proclaim freedom for the prisoners and recovery of sight for the blind, to release the oppressed, to proclaim the year of the Lord's favor.*" (Italics added)

3. A person overwhelmed under an increasingly heavy load

Going through DNX is like being overly burdened and in danger of stumbling and falling. The load feels heavier with each faltering step. "Why would God allow this? Does He see and care what we are going through? Why doesn't God come and help us?"

4. An approaching chariot

DNX is like having a chariot rushing headlong toward us while we are already down on the ground. How do you feel when the person driving the chariot is one who is supposed to care for you—like a parent, loved one, mentor, friend, or mate? What comes to your mind if this is true?

5. **Fleeing from advancing fire**

   DNX is like a dangerous forest fire whipped by out-of-control, wild wind. Our loved ones, reputation, social standing, possessions, and future are threatened without an escape route.

6. **Crossing a flooding river**

   DNX is like bracing against the danger of being carried away by raging floodwater while we dodge hidden, jagged rocks, fallen debris, and snakes underfoot. Paralyzing fear and anxiety are with us along every slippery step of the way.

7. **Place of abundance**

   This last surprising word picture communicates the presence and the purpose of God in our DNX. The picture is that of an oasis in the midst of a desert. It is a wide place, a place of prosperity and purpose, freedom and fruitfulness, restoration and rest. It is a life-affirming destination that God will lead us to at the end of our extreme testing in DNX.

Is there hope for you and me in our DNX? One of the lesser-known acts of King David is recorded in 1 Chronicles 21 in three parts: sin, sacrifice, and sanctuary.

Sin: Satan's evil thought had entered David's heart to trust in his own strength instead of God. David's action of numbering his people resulted in the death of 70,000 people. Instead of looking into the dark abyss of his soul, David looked into the eyes of his heavenly Father and found the life-giving, unfailing love of God. David took responsibility for his sinful act, humbled himself before God, and made necessary restitution.

Sacrifice: David bought the threshing floor of Araunah, where the killing of his people finally stopped. He built an altar and made sacrifices to the Lord.

Sanctuary: Guess what happened to this piece of land? It was later used to build the sanctuary of God (2 Chr 3:1). Every Israelite was aware of its history when they came to worship God.

Was there hope for David when 70,000 people died because of him? Is there hope for you and me when we fail? If God can forgive David and remain present with him, God can do the same for you and me. In spite of our failure and sins or others' faults and mistakes, can God make us into a new sanctuary and point others to worship God? Is a new beginning really possible in Christ? YES. YES. "Tomorrow is always fresh with no mistakes in it" (Anne of Green Gables).[10]

Actions (for personal group study):

1. What surprised you in this chapter? Name three things you gleaned from them.

2. Reflect and write down how each of the seven word pictures relates to your DNX.

---

10   http://anne.sullivanmovies.com/films/anne-of-green-gables.

3. If God could forgive David's sin, would He be able to forgive yours? Memorize 1 John 1:9 and reflect on its promise to you.

4. Ask God to also help you identify and forgive those who have sinned against you. God's forgiveness is instantaneous. Your forgiveness of others may take time and practice to become a reality. Be patient and do not give up!

5. Continue reading the gospel of John and review all three memory verses daily: Proverbs 4:23, Isaiah 41:10, and 1 John 1:9. Ask God to reveal Himself to you through these verses.

CHAPTER **4**

The Grief of Not Understanding
the Dark Night Experience

How do we make sense and give meaning and purpose to
our pain and suffering in DNX? Read on and find out more of
what DNX is all about.

James Dobson defined DNX as "a crisis brewed in the pit of
hell."[11]

St. John of the Cross described DNX as "bitter and terrible"
and "horrible and awful."[12]

Testimony of Henri Nouwen: "This book is my secret journal.
It was written during the most difficult period of my life, from
December 1987 to June 1988. There was a time of extreme
anguish, during which I wondered whether I would be able to
hold on to my life. Everything came crashing down—my self-
esteem, my energy to live and work, my sense of being loved,

---

11   James Dobson. *When God Doesn't Make Sense* (Wheaton: Tyndale House
     Publishers, 1993), 26.
12   St. John of the Cross, *Dark Night of the Soul* (Grand Rapids: Christian Classics
     Ethereal Library, 2000), 28-29.

my hope for healing, my trust in God ... everything. Here I was, a writer about the spiritual life, known as someone who loves God and gives hope to people, flat on the ground and in total darkness.

"What had happened? I had come face to face with my own nothingness. It was as if all that had given my life meaning was pulled away and I could see nothing in front of me but a bottomless abyss.

"The strange thing was that this happened shortly after I had found my true home. After many years of life in universities, where I never felt fully at home, I had become a member of L'Arche, a community of men and women with mental disabilities. I had been received with open arms, given all the attention and affection I could ever hope for, and offered a safe and loving place to grow spiritually as well as emotionally. Everything seemed ideal. But precisely at that time I fell apart—as if I needed a safe place to hit bottom!

"Just when all those around me were assuring me they loved me, cared for me, appreciated me, yes, even admired me, I experienced myself as a useless, unloved, and despicable person. Just when people were putting their arms around me, I saw the endless depth of my human misery and felt that there was nothing worth living for. Just when I had found a home, I felt absolutely homeless. Just when I was being praised for my spiritual insights, I felt devoid of faith. Just when people were thanking me for bringing them closer to God, I felt that God had abandoned me. It was as if the house I had finally found had no floors. The anguish completely paralyzed me. I could no longer sleep. I cried uncontrollably for hours. I could not be reached by consoling words or arguments. I no longer had any interest in other people's problems. I lost all appetite for food and could not appreciate the beauty of music, art, or even nature. All had become darkness. Within me there was one long scream coming from a place I didn't know existed, a place full of demons.

"All of this was triggered by the sudden interruption of a friendship. Going to L'Arche and living with very vulnerable people, I had gradually let go of many of my inner guards and opened my heart more fully to others. Among my many friends, one had been able to touch me in a way I had never been touched before. Our friendship encouraged me to allow myself to be loved and cared for with greater trust and confidence. It was a totally new experience for me, and it brought immense joy and peace. It seemed as if a door of my interior life had been opened, a door that had remained locked during my youth and most of my adult life.

"But this deeply satisfying friendship became the road to my anguish, because soon I discovered that the enormous space that had been opened for me could not be filled by the one who had opened it. I became possessive, needy, and dependent, and when the friendship finally had to be interrupted, I fell apart. I felt abandoned, rejected, and betrayed. Indeed, the extremes touched each other.

"Intellectually I knew that no human friendship could fulfill the deepest longing of my heart. I knew that only God could give me what I desired. I knew that I had been set on a road where nobody could walk with me but Jesus. But all this knowledge didn't help me in my pain.

"I realized quite soon that it would be impossible to survive this mentally and spiritually debilitating anguish without leaving my community and surrendering myself to people who would be able to lead me to a new freedom. Through a unique grace, I found the place and the people to give me the psychological and spiritual attention I needed. During the six months that followed, I lived through an agony that seemed never to end. But the two guides who were given to me did not leave me alone and kept gently moving me from one day to the next, holding on to me as parents hold a wounded child.

"To my surprise, I never lost the ability to write. In fact, writing became part of my struggle for survival. It gave me the little distance from myself that I needed to keep from drowning in my despair. Nearly every day, usually immediately after meeting with my guides, I wrote a 'spiritual imperative'—a command to myself that had emerged from our session. These imperatives were directed to my own heart. They were not meant for anyone but myself.

"In the first weeks it seemed as if my anguish only got worse. Very old places of pain that had been hidden to me were opened up, and fearful experiences from my early years were brought to consciousness. The interruption of friendship forced me to enter the basement of my soul and look directly at what was hidden there, to choose, in the face of it all, not death but life. Thanks to my attentive and caring guides, I was able day by day to take very small steps toward life. I could easily have become bitter, resentful, depressed, and suicidal. That this did not happen was the result of the struggle expressed in this book.

"When I returned to my community, not without great apprehension, I reread all I had written during the time of my 'exile.' It seems so intense and raw...But when, eight years later, prompted by my friend...I read my secret journal again, I was able to look at that period of my life and see it as a time of intense purification that had led me gradually to a new inner freedom, a new hope, and a new creativity." [13]

Dr. R. T. Randall was of the opinion that "100 percent of the believers eventually go through a period when God seems to let them down. ... More than 90 percent of us [will] fail to break through..."[14] Trebesch of Fuller Seminary reported that in "over 1000 case studies of leaders in the School of World Mission leadership concentration[,] [a]bout 95% of these have one or more isolation experiences as shaping factors in their lives."[15]

Many names but the same experience

Other common terms used to describe DNX are "dark night of the soul" (St. John of the Cross), "the valley of the shadow of death," "hitting the wall," "the darkest moon," "isolation," "desert," "wilderness," "tunnel," "valley experience," "crisis of faith," "winter of the heart," "the ministry of the night,"[16] "the child of the light walking in darkness,"[17] etc.

---

13 Henri J.M. Nouwen. *The Inner Voice of Love: A Journey Through Anguish to Freedom* (New York, NY: Image Books, 1998), xiii-xvii.

14 Dobson, *Sense*, 26, 28

15 Shelly G. Trebesch. *Isolation: A Place of Transformation in the Life of a Leader* (Altadena: Barnabas Publishers, 1997), 56

16 www.sermonaudio.com/sermoninfo.asp?SID-8509163412

17 Charles H. Spurgeon, "The Child of Light Walking in Darkness, Sermon No. 1985, " downloaded from www.spurgeongems.org/vols31-33/chs1985.pdf.

Theologians call it "Deus Absconditus"—the God who is hidden.[18] Jesus experienced it on the cross as He called out, "My God, my God, why have you forsaken me?" (Mt 27:46).

There are eight prominent characteristics of DNX.

1. **Loss**—Every Dark Night Experience involves loss. The greater the loss, the deeper the grief. The reality and sense of loss encompasses the past, the present, and the future.

2. **Abandonment**—The sense of being abandoned by God is that "special darkness, the darkness that is the most fearsome of all to the child of God[,] the divine darkness … of the withdrawn sense of the presence of God."[19] Whether real or perceived, the pain from being left behind and forgotten is unmistakably personal and acute and it leaves indelible tracks in and throughout one's life journey.

3. **Alone and lonely**—Phillip Yancey wrote, "people, who are suffering, whether from physical or psychological pain, often feel an oppressive sense of aloneness. They feel abandoned, by God and also by others, because they must bear the pain alone and no one else quite understands. Loneliness increases the fear, which in turn increases the pain, and downward the spiral goes."[20] We are most vulnerable to depression and despair in this state of isolation.

---

18   Ron Dunn. *When Heaven is Silent: How God Ministers to Us Through the Challenges of Life* (Milton Keynes: Authentic Publishing, 1994), 126
19   Winkie Pratney. *The Thomas Factor* (Old Tappan: A Chosen Book, 1989),155-6.
20   Yancey, *Hurts*, 173.

4. **Agony**—Emotional upheaval naturally accompanies devastation and pain. Peter was in agony after he denied Jesus three times and subsequently "went outside and wept bitterly" (Mt 26:74-75). One word of caution here—never, and I mean never, make major decisions in your life with a troubled heart. In several occasions during my DNX I had asked myself, "Is this worth it?" What I was actually saying in my heart was, "I don't really need this. Is walking with God and doing His will worth all these troubles and hassles?" For my wife, her question was, "Can I trust God again with my life and my loved ones?" Others may ask, "Is God going to put me on the shelf?" Someone else may wonder, "Can I keep on trusting God when He does not guarantee me a pain-free future?" Maybe the right question is the one Elizabeth Elliot asked, "Is God worth it?"

5. **Anger** with guilt, fear and anxiety—In times of grief, our minds inevitably turn to seek reasons for our loss. We may become angry when we think someone or something has caused our pain, or we are angry with someone who could or should but did not intervene and we suffer as a result. We feel guilty because our own actions or inactions contribute to our loss and we are unable to undo the damage. We worry about being found out and held responsible.

6. **Confusion**—In the dark we quickly become confused, disoriented, and easily paralyzed with fear and anxiety. According to Dobson, "Sooner or later, most of us will come to a point where it appears that God has

lost control—or interest—in the affairs of people. It is only an illusion, but one with dangerous implications for spiritual and mental health. Interestingly enough, pain and suffering do not cause the greatest damage. Confusion is the factor that shreds one's faith... It is the absence of meaning that makes their situation so intolerable."[21] Dobson also observes that, "many people who want to serve the Lord are victimized by a terrible lie that distances them from the Giver of Life. Satan is, as we know, both 'father of lies' (Jn 8:44) and 'a roaring lion looking for someone to devour' (1 Pt 5:8)."[22] Likewise, Patterson notes, "For you and me, in the final analysis, it is not the cancer that confronts us, or the divorce, or the loss of a job, or nuclear holocaust—it is God."[23]

7. **Knowing and not knowing**—Deep in the pit of our stomach fear grips our soul. We *know* we are way out of our depth in this darkness and despair. We *know* that we do not *know* what is going on and what we are doing. We are grasping at straws that repeatedly dash our hope. Life as we *know* it is slipping out of our grip. We feel lost and overwhelmed, *knowing* nothing of the experiences and emotions that are staring us in the face.

8. **Setbacks**—In DNX we are confronted with successive setbacks over lengthy periods of time. The fact that we might have to start up life again, from the bottom

---

21 Dobson, *Sense*, 13-14.
22 Ibid., 28.
23 Ben Patterson. *Waiting: Finding Hope When God Seems Silent* (Downers Grove: InterVarsity Press, 1989), 27.

rung, is profoundly humiliating and makes us feel vulnerable. Any remaining self-confidence or sense of hope is now shredded and shattered.

Actions (for personal and group study):

1. How does Nouwen's testimony add to your understanding of DNX?

2. Rank the 8 characteristics that best relate to your DNX right now and why?

3. Write down and give thanks to God for 10 things in your life.

4. A friend said to me before I left college on my way to being drafted into the military during the Vietnam War, "John, never stop asking for forgiveness." (I wonder what he knew about me.) Is this saying true for you, too? Why is it so hard to keep coming back to God for forgiveness?

5. List three things you have gleaned from the study thus far.

CHAPTER 5

The Grief of Not Understanding How the Dark Night Experience Unfolds

David's DNX—"Save me, O God, for the waters have come up to my neck. I sink in the miry depths, where there is no foothold. I have come into the deep waters; the floods engulf me. I am worn out calling for help; my throat is parched. My eyes fail, looking for my God" (Ps 69:1-3).

Testimony: A seminarian shared with me the following comments after she heard me preach on DNX from the life of Job. "Now I know all the emotions and struggles that I went through after the death of my brother three years ago were legitimate and normal. I was feeling guilty about how badly I reacted. I now realize God cares and He was in the midst of my Dark Night Experience. I am ready to accept what happened and move on with my life from now on."

From my journal—"I am in an impossible situation and remain inconsolable in this darkness. I am incapable of getting out of this darkness. I am totally inadequate in dealing with this darkness."

The following is an example of how DNX unfolds in a life in the book of Job.

Job's DNX—"Yet when I hoped for good, evil came; when I looked for light, then came darkness. The churning inside me never stops; days of suffering confront me" (Jb 30:26-27).

Chronologically, the Book of Job is the first book of the Bible. Guess what the theme of the book is about? It is all about DNX and the sovereignty of God.

Can you imagine what it must have been like for Job, the Bill Gates of his times, when he realized, "What I feared has come upon me; what I dreaded has happened to me." (Jb 3:25)? Job curses the day he was born four times in one chapter (Jb 3: 2-3, 7-8, 22). He uses the word *dark* or *darkness* 26 times to describe his anguish. "I have no peace, no quietness; I have no rest, but only turmoil" (3:26). Job's DNX stuns all his senses yet unfolds right under the watchful eyes of the sovereign and almighty God.

Job, "a blameless and righteous man" according to God, is struggling for his life and faith. God, seemingly, is not answering his prayers and questions. When Job needs Him the most, God is nowhere to be found. Job is helplessly and hopelessly stuck in confusion, agony, and pain for 35 long chapters. From Job's experience I observed seven distinct stages and processes.

I. Stripping Away (like the polished arrow in chapter 1)— the loss (Jb 1:1-19)

Here are some of Job's losses that produce deep anguish in his soul:

- The death of his ten children; total destruction of properties; loss of reputation, possessions, health, friends, the support of his wife, respect, good works, etc.

- The loss of will to continue living, regretting that he was ever born. (Jb 3:1-3, 7-8, 22).

- Finding no one who understands and is able to empathize with his pain. Instead, Job is falsely accused and condemned by his friends for causing his own suffering.

- Even God seems to be lost to him as Job searches for reasons to explain his loss to himself and others. Who can take this kind of loss all at one time?

II. Worship (Jb 1:20-2:22)

Amazingly, Job's immediate response to his herculean loss is worship. Job is living up to his reputation as a blameless man who fears God. "Job got up and tore his robe and shaved his head. Then he fell to the ground in worship and said: 'Naked I came from my mother's womb, and naked I will depart. The LORD gave and the LORD has taken away; may the name of the LORD be praised'" (Jb 1:20-21). What an insightful understanding of life and loss!

A second worshipping experience follows after God allows Satan to touch his body with painful boils from head to toe. "His wife said to him, 'Are you still holding on to your integrity? Curse God and die!' He replied, 'You are talking like a foolish woman. Shall we accept good from God, and not trouble?' In all this, Job did not sin in what he said" (Jb 2:9-10). Job is acknowledging that God knows what He is doing and has the right to give and take away. Job's response was once again to worship.

Don't be too hard on Job's wife for her seemingly crude comment. Wrestling with her own grief of loss, she is also facing the toughest grief of all—the grief of losing hope as she helplessly witnesses her husband's agony and pain in his suffering. (I will explain this more in chapter 9.) Up to this point, Job "did not sin" in either charging God for wrongdoing or in what he had to say (Jb 1:22, 2:10b). For seven days and nights his three friends sat with him in total silence. But "after this, Job opened his mouth" (Jb 3:1) and out came a flood of questions, laments, anguish, confusion, and declarations that must have been building up inside him till they overflowed.

III. Wrestling

We cannot ascertain how much time passed between the onset of disasters and the opening of dialogues among friends. But the sheer volume of words in 35 chapters describes Job's intensely painful wrestling with many tormenting questions (Jb 34:5-6; 13:14, 15; 21:7-9) and the silence of God (Jb 3:25, 26; 6:1, 2; 7:11, 16; 9:21; 10:1, 15; 12:4; 19:17-20; 23:1; 27:2; 30:25).

The focus of Job's struggle is not so much with his losses, but mainly with God, His attributes, and His ways. In his intense yearning for relief and understanding Job maintains his confidence in God and his insistence on finding answers in God. "To God belong wisdom and power; counsel and understanding are his" (Jb 12:13). Expressing his dissatisfaction with the rhetoric of his friends, Job insists that only a direct word from God will settle his quest. To his friends, Job says, "My eyes have seen all this, my ears have heard and understood it. What you know, I also know; I am not inferior to you. But I desire to speak to the Almighty and to argue my case with God. ... Why do I put myself in jeopardy and take my life in my hands? Though he slay me, yet will I hope in him; I will surely defend my ways to his face" (Jb 13:1-2, 14-15).[24]

IV. Encounter with God

Now we come to the fourth stage, where Job encounters God twice (Jb 38:1-40:1; 41:6-34). Instead of answering Job's "why" questions, God turns the table and throws out a long series of questions to Job. These questions from God can be summarized into two "who" questions.

- Who are you (Job)? Where were you (Job) when I (God) created the world?

- Who am I (God)? Did you (Job) give me counsel in my creation?

God is breaking His silence. Job's request for an audience has been granted. As he eagerly presents his complaints to God, Job is confident that he will be vindicated for all the terrible things that happened to him. As it turns out, it is Job who is left without a rebuttal. Job's answer to God's questions regarding creation is obviously a resounding "no."

---

24   Cf., Trebesch, *Isolation*, 40

V. Acknowledgement of Job

Job is coming to his senses and seeing his place as a mere creature before the mighty Creator.

- "I am unworthy—how can I reply to you? I put my hand over my mouth. I spoke once, but I have no answer—twice, but I will say no more." (Jb 40:4-5)

- "I know that you can do all things; no plan of yours can be thwarted. You asked, 'Who is this that obscures my counsel without knowledge?' Surely I spoke of things I did not understand, things too wonderful for me to know. You said, 'Listen now, and I will speak; I will question you, and you shall answer me.' My ears had heard of you but now my eyes have seen you. Therefore I despise myself and repent in dust and ashes" (Jb 42:2-6).

In acknowledging the sovereignty, love, omnipotence, and wisdom of God, all the questions that Job was so insistent on finding answers to no longer concern him. Job is coming to a blessed place of posturing himself with honesty and humility before the living God.

VI. Affirmation by God

Job's friends have been trying hard to defend God and assign guilt to Job. It must be shocking, even to Job, that God is angry with his friends for not speaking what is right as Job has (Jb 42:7-8). As a matter of fact, God instructs Job's friends to offer a burnt offering for their sins. Their healing would only come by Job's prayer for them. God affirms Job's earnest desire to speak *to* Him but finds Job's friends' lofty speech *about* Him inadequate and offensive. What pleases God is "a broken and contrite heart" that seeks His face (Ps 51:17; 27:8).

VII. Transformation of Job

"After Job had prayed for his friends, the LORD made him prosperous again and gave him twice as much as he had before" (Jb 42:10). For Job, the transformation was from brokenness to double blessings.

Keep in mind that this is not the end result for all those who go through a DNX. Some people God transports into His glory and then transforms them, "... Some faced jeers and flogging, while still others were chained and put in prison. They were stoned; they were sawed in two; they were put to death by the sword. They went about in sheepskins and goatskins, destitute, persecuted, and mistreated—the world was not worthy of them. They wandered in deserts and mountains, and in caves and holes in the ground. These were all commended for their faith, yet none of them received what had been promised. God had planned something better for us so that only together with us would they be made perfect" (Heb 11:36-40). One thing is for sure— all of us will be changed by our DNX, whether we become bitter, better, or best.

Actions (for personal and group study):

1. What surprised and shocked you about Job's experience?

2. What lessons and questions do you have from this chapter about God, yourself, and life?

3. Memorize 1 Peter 5:10 and reflect on this outline: grief, God, grace, glory, and guarantees (from God to you).

CHAPTER **6**

The Grief of Not Knowing How We End Up in the Dark Night Experience

Here are eight descriptive *E* words that trace how Elijah finds himself in the mess of his DNX (1 Kgs 18). Observe his fears, wounded pride, excuses, and ingenious way of framing his explanation to make himself look good. Observe the gentle and gracious ways God deals with Elijah.

1. **Experience:** All of us have our individual experiences in life and have learned certain guiding principles that have shaped how we live our lives. Like Frank Sinatra and the title of one of his songs, "I Did it My Way," many of us run our lives in a similar way. From 1 Kings 17-18 we learn that Elijah was a great prophet during the reign of the worst of all Israel's kings, King Ahab. Through Elijah, God withheld rain from the land, sustained a widow and her son during famine, raised the dead, and later brought fire down from heaven. In spite of all the positive experiences and even miraculous happenings in his life time, like many of us, Elijah was not prepared for the DNX that was to come next.

2. **Expectation:** All of us carry expectations from our past experiences, both consciously and unconsciously, of what we think life should look like. Some of our expectations are legitimate, biblical, and realistic, and some are not. After Elijah scored an impressive victory over the 450 Baal prophets on Mount Carmel (1 Kgs 18), he had every reason to feel optimistic about his future. But it was not to be so. Just like the main character in the movie *Natural*, Roy Hobbs, said, "Life never turns out the way you expected." And what is the reason?

According to David Roper, it is because Elijah's expectation was unrealistic. As a result, "Elijah's unrealistic expectations led to disappointment. Disappointment, brooded over, bred self-pity, which, indulged in, made him blue. Disillusion is the child of illusion."[25] In *The Screwtape Letters*, C. S. Lewis observed the same when he wrote, "Whatever men expect, they soon come to think they have a right to; the sense of disappointment can ... be turned into a sense of injury."[26] This is true in our DNX when our illusions and expectations of life are shattered and we struggle with experiences of disappointment, despair, discouragement, and depression. Here were some of my expectations that needed revising and reshaping:

-   I have a tendency to jump from problems to seeking solutions based on my limited experiences and resources. This approach to life inevitably drives me to desperation, despair, and discouragement because life is too complex for what I have to offer.

25 David Roper. *The Strength of a Man: Encouragement for Today* (Grand Rapids: Discovery House Publishers, 1989), 152.
26 Dunn, *Silent*, 115.

- I have a *my* and *me* mentality: my life, my kingdom, my world, and *what about me,* and *all about me.* I silently demand or expect others to revolve life around me and my interests according to my timetable and my way.

- I tend to make my good *gifts* from God into my *gods.* Once I was angry at God but did not know why. Later, I realized my arrogant audacity when I challenged God in my mind, "I am mad because you, God, did not ask for my permission before letting this terrible situation happen to me. How dare you do this to me?"

- I discovered that I only feel good about myself when others praise me and when things go my way. I am not really in control of my life but others' opinions and circumstances are.

- I was not aware that I was communicating to others the attitude of *don't tell me what is wrong with me.* So I just kept making the same mistakes.

- At some point in my life, I finally got the message that I could not change or control anyone except myself. If I insist on trying, I only drive others away and myself insane. It is so easy to have an *I care therefore I control* attitude. I used to spend an enormous amount of time promoting myself, convincing others of my goodness, and justifying my faults and mistakes. One of the best decisions I ever made was to confront my shortcomings and be changed by the grace of God. My rationale was that I would rather know my mistakes and be humiliated for awhile so that I can make corrections instead of continuing to reap the bitter fruit of my repeated mistakes.

- I was looking at life through the wrong end of the telescope. I evaluated God and His way through my painful circumstances. As a result, God always turned out to seem unloving, uncaring, and inept. I had to choose to look at my painful experiences through the lens of God's attributes as revealed in Scripture. God remains sovereign, loving, omnipresent, and wise, deserving my trust and obedience regardless of how I feel or what I am experiencing.

- I have a tendency to judge events/people/God prematurely, much like judging a half-finished painting, sculpture, or building. So I have learned not to judge God too soon in my DNX until I press forward and through to the finished product.

- Lastly, I had a naïve expectation that being faithful to God guaranteed me a life of bliss. Bad things should never happen to good people. This unrealistic, wishful thinking went up in smoke when confronted by the harshness of life. My faith in God and views of others and myself were shattered but remolded into a more biblical understanding of life, suffering, and God's unlimited resources for all of life's challenges.

3. **Event (trigger):** "Now Ahab told Jezebel everything Elijah had done ... So Jezebel sent a messenger to Elijah to say, 'May the gods deal with me, be it ever so

severely, if by this time tomorrow I do not make your life like that of one of them. Elijah was afraid and ran for his life.' (1 Kgs 19:1-2)

Because of unrealistic expectations and a warped sense of entitlement, a sudden adverse change in circumstances can easily trigger the onset of a DNX and plunge us into a dark place. We see this being played out in Elijah's life when he became a fugitive triggered by the queen's menacing threat.

4. **Evaluation**: Elijah was at the end of himself. Because he succumbed to the threat on his life and chose to run away, he concluded that he was a failure, unfit to continue serving God. He said to God, "Take my life; I am no better than my ancestors" (1 Kgs 19:4b). I used to think that a triggering event leads directly to experiences of anger, grief, guilt, etc. But no! The result of our evaluation of the event is what gives rise to the emotions in our experience. This is good news, because if we change our evaluation process we can change our emotions.

5. **Emotion**: After the emotional high on Mount Carmel, the vigorous run to meet the king, and news of the queen's threat, Elijah was bone tired and edgy. Fear drove the prophet into the desert and depression took over (1 Kgs 18:45-19:4). As the famous football coach Vince Lombardy once said, "Fatigue makes cowards of us all."

6. **Expression** (outward and inward): In his darkest and most vulnerable moment, fear turned Elijah into a

fugitive and brought to the surface his wounded pride, his unbelief, and his faulty thinking. The most shattering illusions we encounter are often the illusions we have of ourselves. "Sometimes life is one shattered illusion after another, and it is the illusion of ourselves that is the most fragile."[27]

Elijah ran toward God instead of away from God, who did not forsake His prophet in his hour of great need. God provided food, water, and rest for his weary servant. God was committed to walk through the DNX with Elijah. During his journey toward the mountain of God, Elijah began to reflect on what had just happened to him. In framing his story, the prophet knowingly or unknowingly made himself appear to be more honorable and righteous than others. He repeated twice, "I have been very zealous for the LORD God Almighty. The Israelites have rejected your covenant, broken down your altars, and put your prophets to death with the sword. I am the only one left, and now they are trying to kill me too" (1 Kgs 19:10, 14). In gentleness and graciousness God listened patiently to Elijah again and again. Then God revealed to Elijah that, "there are seven thousand in Israel—all whose knees have not bowed down to Baal" (1 Kgs 19:18). These are facts which Elijah was not aware of previously. Elijah's perspective and evaluation of recent events took on new clarity in the light of God's revelation.

Likewise, God does not want us to be stuck in blame, accusations, or excuses that can easily be used as spears to attack others and belittle ourselves and God. In any DNX there are always facts we do not know that are hidden from us.

---

27   Susan Wilson. *Hawkes Cove* (New York: Pocket Books, 2000), 421.

Therefore we need to reserve our judgment and criticism until we see God face to face.

Three options of walking through DNX: the bad, the ugly, and the good.

- **The BAD (the shrink back faith):** We all know what the *bad* is. We say to ourselves, "Since you (God) treat me so terribly, I will not have anything to do with you anymore. I am just going to do what I want and live the way I want." We jump into destructive and addictive behaviors that may temporarily numb our pain but will eventually multiply and prolong our sorrows. These are the ones who *shrink back from faith* (Heb 10:38). A Christian worker once commented, "This particular response of giving up on God in our DNX sounds tempting and easiest at first but it is a dangerous option. This path is filled with potholes and quicksand that ensnare us." This is so very true!

- **The UGLY (the shattered faith):** It is an ugly scene to see people stuck in their prison of bitterness, grief, regrets, revenge, blame, and accusations. This second option may not be our conscious choice at first but eventually an unresolved root of bitterness will sprout a shattered faith. Hebrews 12:15 warns us against the root of bitterness that misses the grace of God in times of testing. "See to it that no one fails to obtain the grace of God, that no root of bitterness springs up and causes trouble, and by it many become defiled." Yes, it is a deadly, contagious disease that taints everyone we touch, especially those who are close to us.

It taints everything we see with doom and gloom. A bitter, grumbling, and critical person is not pleasant to be around. *Are you a bitter, negative, and complaining person?*

- **The GOOD (the stand-firm faith), the best option:** This option is the hardest and the most challenging, but the most rewarding in the long run. It is the choice of entrusting ourselves to God in the midst of not knowing and not understanding. It takes grace and true grit to press on in Christ. Hebrews 10:35-38 points out four reasons to stand firm:

  1. "So do not throw away your confidence; **it will be richly rewarded**" (35).

  2. "You need to **persevere** so that when you have done the will of God, you **will receive what he has promised**" (36).

  3. "For in just a very **little while**, 'He who is coming will come and will not delay'" (37).

  4. "But my **righteous** one will live by faith" (38).

7. **Encounter and embrace** God, self, others, evil, and realities

The following points summarize what we learn about God and Elijah's encounter with God:

In his DNX Elijah ran toward God instead of away from God.

God never once condemned or criticized Elijah for running away and asking to die. Instead, God provided Elijah with sleep, food, and drink for the journey to Horeb (1 Kgs 19:5-8), a "40 days and nights" journey of 70 miles, the distance of two Boston Marathons.

God was never harsh but probed gently with the question, "What are you doing here?"

God embraced Elijah in his emotional outbursts and even verbal abuses. Likewise God wants us to be open and honest with Him without shame or fear. In His sovereign mercy, God even chooses to be maligned and misunderstood by not addressing our complaints at our timing.

Eventually, God reached out for a deep heart-to-heart dialogue when Elijah was ready. When God did speak, not in the wind, earthquake, or fire but in a "gentle whisper," Elijah was able to hear it (1 Kgs 19:11-13). In the same way, God allows us time to reflect, process, and resolve any nagging issues the Dark Night stirs up in our hearts and minds. God is not in a hurry and yet "does not willingly bring affliction or grief to the children of men" for no good reason or purpose (Lam 3:33). Why is God silent at times in our Dark Night Experience? I believe it is because we may not be ready to listen in the vortex of our emotional turmoil. Our heart needs to be purified for the encounter. "Blessed are the pure in heart, for they will see God" (Mt 5:8). God's timetable and His perspective on time are beyond our grasp. Moses spent 40 years in the wilderness. Joseph was imprisoned for 13 years. Abraham and Sarah waited 25 years for their only child. God will speak, but at His timing. We need a childlike heart, like young Samuel who said to God, "Speak, for your servant is listening" (1Sm 3:10).

8. **Entering** into God's path with His presence and peace (1Kgs 19:15-17)

It is very affirming to read that Elijah was not cast aside because of his fear and flight but was re-commissioned in God's service (1Kgs 19:15-16). God's gentleness and graciousness in His dealings with us are beyond our wildest imagination and expectation. This is God's grace—pure, marvelous, unlimited, and undeserved through the death and resurrection of Jesus Christ. Only those who have personally experienced this amazing grace can truly be gracious to others. Have you experienced God's grace and forgiveness? Start right now by talking to Jesus honestly and openly about what you are going through and then claim His grace for yourself.

Actions (for personal and group study):

1. What part(s) of Elijah's DNX surprised you?

2. What have you learned about how God dealt with His children?

3. Respond to this **Question**: "How do I trust and obey God again when I feel He has betrayed and abandoned me?"

4. Do you have a tendency to act and frame your situation in a good light like Elijah?

5. Which of the three options of walking through the DNX are you choosing to live in?

6. Meditate on 1 Peter 5:10 and read its context 1 Peter 5: 5-10.

7. Ask God to help you apply to your present circumstances what you learned in this chapter about God, His way, and any unresolved issues you may need to confront.

CHAPTER 7

The Grief of Our Dark Side in a Dark Place

The seventh tormenting grief we face in DNX is that of facing our dark side in the dark place. **T.S. Elliot** said, "Man cannot take too much truth at one time, especially truth about himself."[28] I believe this is the greatest fear that we are forced to face in DNX. We are like a tea bag that only shows its true color in hot water. DNX is the proverbial hot water that reveals who we really are, our very character with all its flaws and blemishes. We must take courage and examine our lives; as Plato said, "An unexamined life is a life not worth living."

C S Lewis revised his previous book *The Problem of Pain* after the death of his wife. When introducing the newly revised book *A Grief Observed*, his stepson wrote, "In a sense it is not a book at all; it is, rather, the passionate result of a brave man turning to face his agony and examine it in order that he might further understand what is required of us in living this life in which we can expect the pain and sorrow of loss of those whom we love.

---

28 Dunn. *Silent,* 37.

" … This book … is a stark recounting of one man's studied attempts to come to grips with and in the end defeat the emotional paralysis of the most shattering grief of his life.…

"….When Jack [C. S. Lewis] was racked with the emotional pain of his bereavement, he also suffered the mental anguish resulting from three years of living in constant fear, the physical agony of osteoporosis and other ailments, and the sheer exhaustion of spending those last few weeks in constant caring for his dying wife. His mind stretched to some unimaginable tension far beyond anything a lesser man could bear; he turned to writing down his thoughts and his reactions to them, in order to try to make some sense of the whirling chaos that was assaulting his mind."[29]

In his anguish, Lewis himself wrote, "Meanwhile, where is God? This is one of the most disquieting symptoms. When you are happy, so happy that you have no sense of needing Him, if you turn to Him then with praise, you will be welcomed with open arms. But go to Him when your need is desperate, when all other help is vain and what do you find? A door slammed in your face and a sound of bolting and double bolting on the inside. After that, silence. You may as well turn away."[30]

Our dark side

In Hebrews 12:1 the author exhorts us to "*throw off* everything *that hinders* and the sin that so easily *entangles*" in order to run the race marked out for us. In the English Standard

---

29   C.S. Lewis. *The Complete C.S. Lewis Signature Classics* (San Francisco: HarperCollins, 2002), 439, 441.
30   C. S. Lewis, *A Grief Observed*; quoted in Philip Yancey, *Where Is God When It Hurts?* (Grand Rapids: Zondervan, 1990), 15.

Version, the words used are to "lay aside every *weight,* and sin which *clings* so closely." (italics added) DNX exposes at least eight instances of the clinging *weight* and *sin*—our dark side—that hinder and entangle our progress in the dark place. In order to press through our DNX we need to examine these besetting weights one by one:

A fatal flaw: inferiority and superiority complexes

There are many of us who have a self-absorbed propensity for inferiority and superiority complexes, the two sides of the same coin. We hold ourselves as the center of the universe, with a sense of entitlement and murky expectations that spurn instruction and correction (Prv 1:7). Without confronting our pride and self-rightness and becoming teachable, our progress through the DNX will be stalled. It is much like the generation of Israelites who refused to listen to God's instructions and ended up circling the desert for 40 years without entering the Promised Land. With humility and vulnerability, we need to let God's light enter the dark places in our lives so that we may throw off habits and mindsets that entangle and keep us from moving forward.

A toxic person

- There are toxic people in churches, work places, and homes. *Who are they? Am I one?*

- A toxic person is in the habit of fixing blame and accusing others of wrongdoing.

- A toxic person inflicts hurt and pain and then makes

others feel responsible for their abusive behavior. To survive and keep peace at any cost, the abused one has to admit to every infraction. "It is my fault. I should be punished for it. I deserve your angry outburst."

- There may be remorse after the outburst, but the toxic person does not change and will likely re-offend again and again.

- The toxic person seeks to control others through bullying, intimidation, and manipulation. They belittle and despise those who subsequently succumb to their cruel tactics.

- There are four things a toxic person/abuser uses to keep others under their control: lies, omissions, secrets, and isolation.

- The abuser has well-rehearsed and embellished stories to justify his/her actions.

- A toxic person may be a product of a toxic and painful past that has not been properly dealt with. The saying "hurting people hurt people" is very true. "For where you have envy and selfish ambition, there you find disorder and every evil practice" (Jas 3:16). To break this destructive cycle of hurts requires just one person taking the steps to make changes.

Abusers are hard to identify, heartrending to confront, and even harder to get away from. It may take years for the abused to realize the depth of their emotional, spiritual, and physical pain and bondage. Sooner or later, to continue living or working with a toxic person is no longer a viable option. The first step may require the hard decision of distancing oneself from the abuser. This can be a crippling and guilt-ridden experience, especially if the abuser is one who is supposed to love and protect you, like a parent or spouse. Nevertheless, stand firm in your resolve! Be prepared for the backlash of more intense hatred and destructive retaliation. Do not be swayed by the abuser's lure with statements like, "I am the victim" or "look at all the things I have done for you," or "I am going to change." God is not pleased or glorified when we allow ourselves to be tormented by the degrading and subversive tactics of a toxic person. It is our birthright as children of God to live in wholeness and dignity in Christ.

Insatiable thirsts

We are created by and for God (Col 1:16) with thirsts that inform and shape our humanity, e.g. intimacy, significance, security, self-worth, etc. (I hope to address these thirsts in more detail in a later book.) God is intended to be our spring of living water that quenches our thirsts. When we devise our own ways to meet these God-sized needs, we will be sure to come away disappointed and more thirsty than ever. Our self-made effort is like digging a broken well that cannot hold water (Jer 2:13). With our thirsts unmet we are like someone driving a car that is running on empty and going nowhere. "Consider then and realize how ... bitter it is for you when you forsake the LORD your God" (Jer 2:19b).

Poisonous GAS

We all wrestle with guilt, grief, anger, anxiety, and shame (GAS) at different times in our lives. In DNX these negative emotions are magnified to demand our attention every waking moment. Without careful examination and deliberate confrontation, we will find ways to numb or dump them with disastrous consequences that keep us living in our dark places.

Building our own fire

"Who among you fears the LORD and obeys the word of his servant? Let him who walks in the dark, who has no light, trust in the name of the LORD and rely on his God. But now, all you who light fires and provide yourselves with flaming torches, go, walk in the light of your fires and of the torches you have set ablaze" (Is 50:10-11a).

It is human nature to want to be in control, to plot our destiny, and to feel competent to take care of ourselves. We feel threatened when we encounter situations that seem far beyond our ability to cope. Every one of us despises the feeling of helplessness and inadequacy. We attempt to build our own fire to escape the darkness and the dread, but often end up jumping from the frying pan into the fire. Having been promised an heir 10 years before, Sarah, Abraham's wife, remained barren. In their impatience and desperation, they made their own fire by agreeing to let Hagar the maidservant be a surrogate mother (Gn 16), which birthed a sibling rivalry that still exists millennia later (Gn 21:1-21).

In 2 Corinthians 1:8, Paul and his team were under great pressure "far beyond [their] ability to endure." They were in danger of losing hope and "despaired even of life." This is the feeling of helplessness and hopelessness. Surprisingly, this turns out to be the best thing that can ever happen to us. The apostle Paul testified that their experience caused them, "not [to] rely on [themselves] but on God, who raises the dead" (1:9). Learning to trust God in "far beyond" situations takes us into God and His unlimited resources. But to begin this journey we have to surrender our control to God. "The biggest block to our surrender is not our appetites and wayward desires, but our addiction to running our own lives."[31] "Beware of turning to evil, which you seem to prefer to affliction" (Job 36:21).

Lack of self-control with our body, soul, and spirit

Another aspect of our lives in DNX that needs careful examination may be our lack of self-control and discipline, as in gluttony, drunkenness, daydreaming, gossiping, addiction, perversion, etc. "Like a city whose walls are broken down is a man who lacks self-control" (Prv 25:28). Left unprotected, all areas of our lives are vulnerable to pillaging by the Enemy of our soul, who seeks "to steal and kill and destroy" our birthright and inheritance in Christ (Jn 10:10).

Drifting spiritually

Drifting spiritually is one reason our darkness may not lift.[32] It

---

31   Gary L. Thomas. *Seeking the Face of God* (Eugene: Harvest House Publishers, 1994) 91.
32   John Piper, *When the Darkness Will Not Lift: Doing What We Can While We Wait for God—and Joy* (Wheaton: Crossway Books, 2006), 23, 64.

is effortless to drift in the dark. I always say, "If you don't know where you are going, you will end up where you don't want to be." For the darkness to lift we need to drop anchor, resolve to take steps to allow God to examine our lives, and lean in to lay hold of God's unconditional love and abundant grace for us. *"Search me, O God, and know my heart; test me and know my anxious thoughts. See if there is any offensive way in me, and lead me in the way everlasting"* (Ps 139:23-24).

Temptation to pursue performance, possessions and popularity

In Matthew 4:1-11 Jesus was tempted to prove His divine Sonship on Satan's terms regarding pride, performance, possessions, position, and popularity. In today's society, people are tempted in the same way to pursue these elusive dreams at all cost, climbing the ladder of success only to find the ladder leaning on the wrong wall when they reach the top.

Actions (for personal and group study):

1. Is it hard to face your dark side in a dark place and why?

2. Read again the propensity we all have toward certain sins and bad habits. Which ones of these eight are you most vulnerable to right now and why?

3. Ask God to give you the will to break from your past and bad influences and to start anew with God. Ask Him to forgive your sins and to create in you a new heart. Ask the Holy Spirit to fill you with Himself and His Word for your journey forward.

4. Memorize and meditate on Psalm 32:8-9. God promises us that He will teach us principles, instruct us how to put them into practice, and guide us as we apply them to our situation.

5. Give thanks to God for His unfailing love and guidance even though you might not understand its full extent yet.

CHAPTER 8

The Grief of Evil, Suffering, and God

"I'd rather be in this wheelchair with God than on my feet without Him. In heaven I look forward to folding up my wheelchair, handing it to Jesus, and saying straight from the heart, 'Thanks, I needed that.'"[33] — **Joni Eareckson Tada, author and disability advocate**

The problem of evil, suffering, and God

"One of the darkest and most mysterious valleys of human existence [is] the problem of suffering and sorrow."[34] "No matter who you are, this is one of the most significant questions you will ever face. It is a crucial question for Christians. When unanswered, it can leave tremendous doubts, or even anger and resentment against God. Some Christians have become overwhelmed at the thought of a good God allowing evil to destroy men. With mounting confusion and frustration, many no longer follow the Lord. ... We can't be good spiritual warriors without

---

33 Schuller, *Halos,* 158.
34 Paul E. Billheimer. *Don't Waste Your Sorrows* (Fort Washington: Christian Literature Crusade, 1977), 16

having the answer to this question. We can't stand against evil and pray confidently for its removal if we don't know why it's here. We cannot have absolute confidence in God unless we are sure of His innocence when it comes to evil in the earth today."[35]

I will attempt to lay out for you the result of my own wrestling through this eighth grief regarding evil, suffering, and God. It is not *the* answer to the problem of pain and suffering, but only God's answers to me for my encouragement and quest.

The theological, Biblical, and logical approach

The problem of pain and suffering is a complex topic that requires a multi-disciplinary approach in order to gain a firm handle. Theological, biblical, and logical/rational acumen all need to be on hand to cull insights and answers to this critical question of suffering and Dark Night Experience.

One of the most frequently asked questions concerning suffering is "why?" "'Why did my nephew get hit by a car?' 'Why did my wife have a stroke?' 'Why did I give birth to a deformed child?' 'Why did such a good person have to die?' The real question is, 'Why did God allow it?'" For some it may even be more direct: 'Why did God do it?'…. When tragedy strikes, God becomes the villain. Unexplained catastrophes are labeled as an 'act of God.' He is blamed for plague and famine."[36] Even if we do not link God directly with the evil in the world, "as Christians, we [may still] struggle with what seems to be God's complicity in all this. We know He is sovereign. Couldn't He step in and do something? Why doesn't

---

35 Dean Sherman, *Spiritual Warfare For Every Christian* (Seattle: YWAM Publishing, 1990), 127-8.
36 Ibid., 127.

He intervene more? What keeps Him from ending wars, keeping people from tragedy, and instantly making the earth a nice place to live? We make it a mess, but can't He fix it?"[37]

It is clear that most of these "why" questions we wrestle with point to the more foundational and impactful question about God's attributes and ways: If God is a God of love, why is there evil in the world?

1. Complications in answering questions about suffering

Not only is the question of pain and suffering complex, answering the question also poses complications. For one sure fact, God does not give a full explanation about suffering to His people in the Scriptures and He is not obligated to do so.[38] Job discovered that "God ... owed him no explanation for what He was doing with him. Job could lay no demands on God. God is not in Job's, or in anyone else's, debt. He is absolutely and sovereignly free to do whatever he, in his wisdom and power and goodness, deems right. He consults with no one, least of all us."[39]

Nevertheless, we know from the accounts of God's dealings with His people that God is, at the same time, all-loving, gracious, and merciful in all His ways. Testimonies of God's people instill in us encouragement, endurance, and hope, especially in suffering (Rom 15:4). As reassuring as this foundational understanding of God's sovereignty and love can be, it can also be threatening during intense trials and deep sorrow when these two aspects of God's attribute seem to butt heads against each other. In times of prolonged testing and pain,

---

37   Ibid., 129.
38   Dobson, *Sense*, 8.
39   Patterson, *Waiting*, 69.

when God seems silent and absent in spite of our repeated pleading, when the darkness of our Dark Night persists un-abated, when our feeble arms are too weak to hang on to faith in God, when our weak knees are too wearied to take another step in trust, we find our hope in God slipping away. As a result, hope often becomes a casualty and the path to finding answers to one's suffering becomes even more muddled.

Job knew this dilemma well: "The speeches of traumatized Job as he sat among the ashes, sick, bewildered, and hurting in his mind as well as his body, express the death of hope in classic terms. 'My days ... come to an end without hope' (Jb 7:6). 'As water wears away stones and torrents wash away the soil, so you (God!) destroy man's hope' (Jb 14:18-19). 'If the only home I hope for is the grave ... where then is my hope? Who can see any hope for me?' (Jb 17:13-15). 'He (God) uproots my hope like a tree' (Jb 19:10)."[40]

"How then does one proceed to find answers to suffering when hopelessness erodes our confidence in God's sovereignty and love? Can I trust God that there is an answer with Him? Can I trust God that He really is able to work all things for my good? Will I ever see in visible ways that He truly loves me and is for me? What would be the basis for hope to arise again from one's profound sense of hopelessness? For Job, he could receive no basis for hope from God other than 'trust me to know what I'm doing,' which is the message conveyed to him by God's review of some of the cosmic glories and wonderful living creatures he has made" (Jb 38-41).[41]

---

40   J.I. Packer and Carolyn Nystrom. *Never Beyond Hope: How God Touches & Uses Imperfect People.* (Downers Grove: InterVarsity Press, 2000), 19.
41   Ibid., 19.

Like Job, we have to keep on keeping on trusting and believing. Like Simon Peter attested, "Lord, to whom shall we go? You have the words of eternal life" (Jn 6:68). Before we end this section, I want us to consider one important spiritual exercise that will help us stay on course in our journey through the Dark Night. It has to do with a change in expectation in our overall outlook on life.

"Many people sincerely believe that *happiness* is the purpose of life"[42] and expect God, who is all loving and powerful, to be committed to making us happy and prosperous with hassle-free lives. However, God's ultimate purpose in all His doings in our lives and in the world is not to make us happy. Not only does He want to see the whole world saved, but He also wants to make us more Christ-like (Rom 8:28-30). Unless we align our expectations with God's purpose, we will always feel like God is failing us in His promises. In our disappointment, we are easily led astray to take the easy way out, giving up the demanding yet rewarding path of persevering in our faith and trust in God. Remember Joseph who was able to testify to his brothers in retrospect, "You intended to harm me, but God intended it for good to accomplish what is now being done, the saving of many lives" (Gn 50:20).

2. My approach to answering the question of suffering

Being a finite, created human being, I have no right nor am I qualified to make a definitive judgment on why the Creator God allows suffering in the world that He created. To *judge* means to pronounce a verdict and sentence based on what I

---

42 Warren Wiersbe, *Why Us?: When Bad Things Happen to God's People* (Leicester, England: InterVarsity Press, 1984), 20.

know and understand. It is absolutely preposterous for anyone to think that they are capable of knowing all there is to know about everything and everyone in the world. Even the little bit that we know, we only "know in part" because we only "see but a poor reflection as in a mirror" (1 Cor 13:9, 12). As long as we are on this side of eternity, it is prudent of us to acknowledge that suffering and conflict are the norm in a fallen world and Christians are not exempt from them. We can also be certain from the great clouds of witnesses down through the millennia that all who embrace God in their DNX will find God to be true to His character and His Word. The Dark Night Experience is an integral part of a process God uses to equip us to reach the world with the Good News. On that glorious day when we come face to face with God we will join with the multitudes in doxology, marveling at the "depth of the riches of the wisdom and knowledge of God! How unsearchable his judgments, and His paths beyond tracing out!" (Rom 11:33).

In accepting the irrefutable, dark reality of our world, we are nonetheless allowed to wrestle, doubt, and question God in our DNX. Job and Jeremiah cursed the day they were born. The psalmists' laments, doubts, and questionings were recorded and put to music for use in public worship. But at the end of their complaints, the psalmists never failed to affirm their faith and confidence in God as God the Most High who is all wise, loving, and sovereign. The answer to their "why?" questions is always the "who." *Who is this God of the Bible?* All who have ever lived will one day bend their knees and confess with their tongues that God in Christ is truly the Lord of the universe and all human history (Phil 2:10). Willingly or reluctantly, we all will bow before the throne of God and none will have any cause to accuse God of unfairness or injustice.

Concerning natural disasters, wars, and famines, Jesus Himself acknowledged them as part of life in this fallen world and as warnings and reminders of His return and our need to account for how we live our lives on earth (Mt 24:6-8, 42-44). For believers, suffering and adversity are also unmistakable ways to remind us that this world is not our home.

3. My understanding and rationale in the "why, when, and where" question

God declared all that He created to be "good" and His creation of human beings as "very good" (Gn 1). God created human beings, male and female, in His own image with the will and freedom to make choices and decisions. You and I are not robots, but God's image bearers. However, this gift of will and freedom contributes to the problem of suffering as we know it.

- Free will—God placed Adam and Eve in the Garden of Eden with choices. "You are free to eat from any tree in the garden; but you must not eat from the tree of the knowledge of good and evil, for when you eat of it you will surely die" (Gn 2:16-17). Sadly, Adam and Eve chose to disobey God and the rest of the human race suffers the consequences of their rebellion.

- The curse—Through Adam, sin entered the world, and death through sin (Rom 5:12). Creation itself is in bondage to decay (Rom 8:21) and every human being is since born a sinner by nature and a sinner by choice. Sin permeates every part and facet of our personhood and pollutes all relational networks. Nothing escapes the destructive reaches of sin. Natural disasters. Wars and rumors of wars. Crimes and atrocities. Immorality and perversions. *Need I go on?*

- Why is evil still allowed in this world? "Evil is allowed to remain in the earth because free will is more valuable than the absence of evil. ... Without it we would be less than human. Free will is absolutely necessary for the quality of relationship that God wants us to have with Him and with other human beings."[43]

- Satan—Also called the devil. Because Adam and Eve sinned, the world is under the control of the evil one (1Jn 5:19). Satan is referred to as "the prince of this world" (Jn 12:31; 14:30). The name "Satan" means "adversary" who stands in active opposition to God. Satan's agenda is to "steal and kill and destroy" (Jn 10:10a) all that God possesses and His plans in and for His creation. Satan is also called the "devil," which means "accuser." The devil is singled out as "the accuser of our brothers...before our God day and night" (Rv 12:10b), stirring up strife and causing rifts in relationships. The devil is the father of lies and deception is the game he plays to blind people from the truth about God and to keep them under his control and manipulation (Jn 8:44). The devil is also called a "murderer" who holds the power of death through sin to keep in slavery those who fear death (Jn 8:44; Heb 2:14; 1Pt 5:8). Those who know and follow Christ are in this spiritual battle in which Satan is determined to destroy anything and anyone that is of God.

---

43   Sherman, *Spiritual Warfare*, 129.

- Who is responsible for the evil in this world? Even though "a man's own folly ruins his life, [and] yet his heart rages against the LORD" (Prv 19:3), God is not responsible for the evil in this world but remains in perfect control. James 1:13-15 warns, "When tempted, no one should say, 'God is tempting me.' For God cannot be tempted by evil, nor does he tempt anyone; but each one is tempted when, by his own evil desire, he is dragged away and enticed. Then, after desire has conceived, it gives birth to sin; and sin, when it is full-grown, gives birth to death."

- Why does God not do something about the sin and suffering in the world? *God has!* When God created the world He set down natural and moral laws to govern this world. *We reap what we sow* is that irrefutable and unchanging law of cause and effect. Sin has consequences. Suffering results from wrong choices we or others make. God hates suffering, death, and sin, but God loves the people in the world. In love, God took the initiative and became "the chief sufferer in the universe."[44] God paid the ultimate price, the life of His only Son, to make things right with His creation. By His death, and victory over death in resurrection, Jesus destroyed Satan and was able to "free those who all their lives were held in slavery by their fear of death" (Heb 2:15). God makes all things new in the lives of those who are in Christ (2 Cor 5:17). God even prepares in advance the good works we are to do, giving us meaning and purpose in living (Eph 2:10). "There is now no condemnation for those who

---

44   Billheimer, *Don't Waste*, 29.

are in Christ Jesus" (Rom 8:1). Through the death and resurrection of Christ, God, in one decisive stroke, foiled and reversed all the schemes and works of the devil. God is definitely without malice and the motive behind all that He does cannot be anything evil. In and through Christ, God *has* definitely done something about the sin and suffering of the world. Yes, He has indeed. Remember the cross and the empty tomb!

- What do we learn about suffering from the death of Jesus on the cross? Dr. Alister McGrath offers his insight as follows: "Christ's death and resurrection draw the sting out of suffering. They declare that suffering is not meaningless. God worked out the salvation of the world through the suffering of Christ. Suffering does not always result from sin and lead to separation from God; the suffering of the sinless Christ and his resurrection to glory make this point more powerfully than we could ever have hoped. Through faith we are bonded to Christ in a 'fellowship of sharing in his sufferings' (Phil 3:10). And suffering does not mean that this world lies beyond the power or love of God. The Almighty God stooped down in humility to suffer for us, to show us the full extent of his love for us. ... Suffering is defeated, not in the sense of being abolished, but in the sense of being turned around. Suffering, along with its ally death, tries to separate us from God by breaking our links with him and severing our life-giving fellowship with him. But through the Cross suffering has been humiliated. The suffering of Christ proves to be the grounds of our union with God. ... Suffering which was once seen as our enemy, something which separated us from God, can now be seen as something which can bring us closer to God. ... Furthermore, we can rejoice in the sure and certain hope, grounded in the resurrection of Christ and sealed by the Holy Spirit, that one day we shall be delivered from the presence of suffering."[45]

J.I. Packer adds, "[The] heart of the Christian hope, both here and hereafter, is the saved sinner's loving fellowship with the Father, the Son, and the Holy Spirit, worshiping, obeying and using enterprise to please the divine Three by [our] service."[46]

Testimony of Neil Anderson: "My family and I went through a very broken experience. For 15 months I didn't know whether my wife, Joanne, was going to live or die. We lost everything we had. God gave me something very dear to me that I could not fix. No matter what I did, nothing changed. God brought me to the end of my resources, so I could discover His. That was the birth of Freedom in Christ Ministries. Nobody reading this book knows any better than I do that I can't set anybody free; only God can do that. I can't bind up anybody's broken heart; only God can do that. He is the Wonderful Counselor. Brokenness is the key to effective ministry ... Message and method had come together. ... [W]e must start where the Bible starts: We must have a true knowledge of God and know who we are as children of God. If we really knew God, our behavior would change radically and instantly. Whenever heaven opened to reveal the glory of God, individual witnesses in the Bible were immediately and profoundly changed. I believe that the greatest determinant of mental and spiritual health and spiritual freedom is a true understanding of God and a

---

45   Alister E. McGrath. *Suffering & God* (Grand Rapids: Zondervan Publishing House, 1995), 68-69
46   Packer and Nystrom, *Never Beyond Hope*, 22.

right relationship with Him. A good theology is an indispens-able prerequisite to a good psychology." [47]

Actions (for personal and group study):

1. Write out from this chapter what points you agree and/or disagree with and the issues you struggle with.

2. What have you gleaned from this chapter about God and His way? Bring them all to God in prayer.

3. Review all the memory verses so far and list the prom-ises of God in them.

---

47 Neil Andersen, *Victory over Darkness,* 2nd ed. (Ventura: Regal Books, 2000), 17-18

CHAPTER 9

The Grief of Lost Hope

Testimony of Connie Mitchell: "It was dark by the time Scott Mitchell drove out of the church parking lot and headed home. The meeting had been good and the prayer support encouraging, but even quiet praise songs playing over the car stereo couldn't still the turmoil in his spirit. Scott and his wife Connie had tried so many times to help their drug-addicted son. Fresh out of hope, they had one last chance but it hung by a slender thread, 'Oh, God,' Scott had prayed more than once, 'I'll do anything. Please save my boy!'

"A member of the pastoral team at Cedar Mill Bible Church in Portland, Oregon, Scott Mitchell was a gifted counselor and speaker who loved music and practical jokes. After graduation from Prairie Bible College in 1977 he married Connie and began ministry in a small church in Washington State.

"They were eager to start a family, but it was 3½ years before their son Jonathan was born, followed by daughter Sadie. The Mitchells returned to Three Hills, Alberta where Scott became

Dean of Men at Prairie and the arrival of a second son Chad rounded out the family circle. But all was not well.

"Bright, but over-active and constantly in trouble, Jonathan proved to be a challenge. It wasn't until second grade that he was diagnosed with Attention Deficit/Hyperactivity Disorder. The condition was poorly understood at the time and while medication helped him do better at school, the side-effects were extreme. When the Mitchells moved on to graduate school and pastoral ministry in the US, it became necessary to home-school and provide tutors for their son who simply could not cope in a classroom setting.

"His behavior grew dangerous and by the age of 13 he was using alcohol and marijuana. Soon it was methamphetamines. Recalling how she had prayed so long for this child and dedicated him to God even before he was conceived, Connie struggled to understand: 'He was so loved and wanted; why was this happening? We felt like terrible parents and went in all different directions trying to find help.'

"But things only worsened as Jonathan's drug use made him paranoid and delusional. One July day in 2004 Scott found him wandering in the house after overdosing heavily on over-the-counter medications. Doctors in intensive care labored to save the boy's life, telling his parents that even if he survived, he would likely need a liver transplant.

"In desperation they turned to their church family for prayer support and against all odds, Jonathan pulled through. His behavior was still extremely confused and psychotic but he understood that his life was in ruins and needed to change.

After a long search, the Mitchells found a promising treatment program in New Hampshire and hopes rose once more. Then the axe fell. Jonathan was arrested for public disturbance and faced six months in jail.

"His parents had always made it clear that Jonathan would have to face the consequences of his own actions. This time, however, Scott felt compelled to go before the judge and plead for leniency. They had almost lost their son and the New Hampshire program was his last chance. They dared not miss this opportunity. The judge agreed. After giving the boy a stern warning, he sent him home in the custody of his father.

"With so much family stress, Scott and Connie were looking forward to some time away together in New Orleans—until Connie tripped on the stairs and broke her foot. In spite of their disappointment they had no choice but to spend their holidays at home. It was a good week nevertheless, with plenty of time to laugh and enjoy each other's company. On Wednesday evening Scott went to a planning meeting for their men's ministry at the church, leaving Connie resting in bed.

"He came home to find that Jonathan's girlfriend, a fellow addict, had arrived at the house. Knowing what a negative impact she could have on the boy at this crucial time, Scott went downstairs and politely asked her to leave. Soon Connie heard Jonathan's angry voice and the slamming of a door. Moments later another sound made her reach for her crutches and hobble to the head of the stairs.

"Scott had locked the basement door when the young people left, not realizing that Jonathan was barefoot. Nor was he aware that his son's irrational fears had prompted him to buy a small .22 caliber handgun. When he couldn't get back in, Jonathan took the gun in his left hand, smashed the window glass and unlocked the door. Grabbing the shoes, he left without a word, completely unaware that the weapon had discharged.

"Connie discovered her husband standing at the bottom of the stairs in shock with a sinister red stain spreading across his shirt. Realizing he had been shot, she scrambled frantically down the steps and tried to stop the flow of blood while she called 911.

"The lone bullet struck Scott in the collarbone and ricocheted down to penetrate the pulmonary artery. Hemorrhaging uncontrollably, he collapsed on the floor and by the time paramedics arrived, it was too late. Scott Mitchell's life had reached a tragic and untimely end.

"Police fanned out in an area-wide search for the gunman but Jonathan was no-where to be found. Connie, Sadie and Chad spent a sleepless night huddled together in shock and grief. They knew that in his psychotic state Jonathan might very well harm himself once he realized what he had done.

"The next day the boy reappeared out of nowhere, oblivious to the tragedy. Approaching the policemen surrounding the family home, he demanded to know what they were doing there. When he was arrested on the spot, Jonathan's paranoia kicked into high gear. Insisting that he was the victim of a conspiracy, he refused to believe that his father was dead until photos of the crime scene were shown to him.

"Torn between grief for her husband and fear for her son, Connie was in agony. The question that broke her heart wasn't why? but why did it have to be this way? 'I could have been at peace with the fact that it was Scott's time to leave this earth,' she recalls, 'but couldn't it have been a heart attack or a car accident? Why did it have to involve Jonathan?'

"Evidence would later confirm that the shooting was not intentional. Jonathan had no idea the gun had fired until it was proven that the bullet missing from his .22 matched the one that had killed his father. Stunned and devastated, he accepted responsibility and pled guilty, sparing the family the ordeal of a lengthy trial. However, while Jonathan had meant no harm, the fact that he was carrying a weapon while under the influence of drugs indicated a dangerous recklessness. Just 23 years old, he was convicted of manslaughter and sentenced to 11 years in prison. Young Jonathan Mitchell would spend the prime of his life behind bars.

"In the weeks that followed Connie pored over Scott's personal journals. One entry caught her attention: 'When I am tested I will come forth as gold. I may not know where God is in all that is going on, but I know that he is involved.' The scripture that followed was from Isaiah 45: I will go before you and level the mountains; I will break down gates of bronze and cut through bars of iron. I will give you treasures of darkness… that you may know that I am the Lord…

"Treasures? In such darkness? How could that be? It was impossible not to dwell on the fact that the shooting could easily have been prevented. But for her broken foot, Connie and her husband would have been on vacation. If Scott had not intervened with the judge, Jonathan would have been in jail. Had God slipped up?

"Knowing she would drown in the circumstances if she concentrated on the what-ifs, Connie asked God to keep her focused instead on his love and goodness. All her life she had experienced his faithfulness. Now it was time to stand on that foundation. As her focus became a habit, it gradually became possible to pray that God would reveal himself in this tragedy and that her pain would somehow help others who were suffering.

"Feeling that she had some control over her life had always given Connie a sense of security. Now everything had changed without warning and once again there was a choice to be made. Connie began placing both Jonathan and her own future into God's hands, even though she had no idea what the end would be. The result was that 'knowing God was in control gave me hope instead of despair.' Learning to pray by faith was giving her the strength to refuse to worry. The treasures were starting to shine.

"Sleep came fitfully in those first terrible nights. But to Connie's surprise, songs of praise were running through her mind whenever she awoke. Gathering up all her favorite CDs, she played them on the computer all night long and without fail the right words would be there in the darkness exactly when she needed them. On what would have been their 29th wedding anniversary Connie awoke to a special gift from God: a recording of Scott's beautiful voice singing 'Oh, I Want to Know You More.'

"Being immersed continuously in praise was having a profound effect on Connie's spirit. Never before had she experienced such deep pain and sorrow. But at the same time she was finding comfort, peace and joy beyond anything she had ever known. It appeared that the two went hand in hand.

" 'My husband's life was not wasted,' says Connie with conviction. 'I am continually hearing about the ongoing results of his investment in the lives of so many people. I don't believe God will waste his death either. Scott had told friends that he would gladly give his own life if it would make a difference for Jonathan. And our son truly has been given a second chance. He might have gone to the program in New Hampshire but I don't think he would have stayed. Now he has no choice. He finally has a clear mind and is healthy and drug-free and learning to make wise choices.'

" 'God is clearing away my short-sightedness and helping me comprehend that he has a much bigger eternal plan than I can even imagine. He knows the end of the story and some day we will see the whole picture. In the meantime I am content to trust in his goodness and love for my family and for me.'"[48]

There are seven tightening strands that contribute to the loss of hope in our DNX

1. **The first tightening strand** is our doubting of God's love for us and whether He truly is a rewarder of those who seek Him (Heb 11:6).

---

48   Connie Mitchell , "Treasures of darkness", *Servant 81*, September 22, 2009, 12-14.

2. The second tightening strand is unanswered prayer.
For years I misunderstood the purpose of prayer. I
thought prayer was God's way to meet my needs and
wants as well as to relieve my and my loved ones'
pain and suffering. But do you catch the purpose of
prayer in Jesus' promise, "And I will do whatever you
ask in my name, so that the Son may bring glory to the
Father" (Jn 14:13)? It is for the glory of God! Do you
know that whatever brings glory to God always works
out for our very best also? This is the thesis of John
Piper's book *Desiring God*.

Do you know too that there are different shades to God's
"no" answer? In Matthew 15 a Canaanite woman cried out
to Jesus, "Lord, Son of David, have mercy on me! My daughter is suffering terribly from demon-possession" (Mt 15:22).
Surprisingly, Jesus' initial response to the woman is **silence:**
"Jesus did not answer a word" (23a).

The silence of God is particularly difficult when our needs
are so urgent. When God is silent, humans make **assertions,
accusations and assumptions,** like Jesus' disciples who said,
"Send her away, for she keeps crying out after us" (23b). Then
Jesus answered the woman with a "no." "I was sent only to
the lost sheep of Israel. ... It is not right to take the children's
bread and toss it to their dogs" (24-26). Undaunted, the woman humbly responded, "Even the dogs eat the crumbs that
fall from their masters' table" (27). Impressed with her per-
sistent faith, Jesus granted the woman's request (28). In this
incident, Jesus' "no" is more than a straightforward refusal
but also implies a **test,** a **delay,** or a **denial** for a greater and
deeper purpose.

I believe one of the biggest tests of "no" comes to those who are caring bystanders in a loved one's DNX, like Job's wife. She shared Job's experience of the same loss of children, land, reputation, etc.—plus one more. She had to watch helplessly as Job, a good and godly man, suffered agonizing pain from the boils on his whole body. She was probably worn out by wrestling with similar unanswered prayer and tormenting questions. Her inability to intervene and alleviate her husband's suffering must have driven her to cry out to Job, "Are you still holding on to your integrity? Curse God and die" (Jb 2:9). God, our heavenly Father, experienced this same agony as He witnessed Jesus sweating blood in Gethsemane, facing humiliating torture, wearing the crown of thorns, stumbling up toward Golgotha, and hanging in excruciating pain on the cross.

Even though God had the power to end the suffering, He chose to hide His face and close His ears to His beloved Son's "loud cries and tears" (Heb 5:7). Jesus, who knew no sin, willingly and voluntarily suffered and bore our sins and judgment in our place on the cross so that we could be forgiven and set free. Yes, our heavenly Father truly understands the pain of watching our loved ones suffer. Will you let your loving Heavenly Father embrace and comfort you right here and right now?

3. **The third strand is Satan's lies**. Satan's lies create doubt in us about God's Word, character, and wisdom. Satan's agenda is always "to steal and kill and destroy" (Jn 10:10a).

4. **The fourth tightening strand is the *I*.** By now we know

that God's "no" answer to our desperate prayers has much deeper meaning and greater purpose. God wants to reveal to us what we are really like when we do not get our way. It is the "I want" that is being tested and challenged. The Canaanite woman demonstrated a humble and reverent attitude, a persevering spirit, and a biblically inspired response to Jesus' "no," what Jesus called a "great faith." Jesus demonstrated the same humility in the Garden of Gethsemane when He said, "My Father, if it is possible, may this cup be taken from me. Yet not as I will, but as you will" (Mt 26:39). God's "no" to the Apostle Paul's three requests for healing came with a "yes" that promised Paul divine rest, power, and sufficient grace in his DNX. Paul learned to embrace both God's "no" and "yes" and to "boast" and "delight" in his weaknesses (2 Cor 12:7-10).

5. **The fifth strand is the longing to run away from God, life, and the pain.** I think one of the hardest things for us in DNX is to obey Jesus' call, "**Come** to me, all you who are weary and burdened, and I will give you rest. **Take** my yoke upon you and **learn** from me, for I am gentle and humble in heart, and you will find rest for your souls. For my yoke is easy and my burden is light" (Mt 11:28-30).

In our DNX, we are desperate for our wearied and burdensome struggles to go away for good through any means. We find ways to escape the painful reality of life instead of turning to God for rest, healing, and comfort. Sadly, "those who trust in chariots and horses are brought to their knees and fall. But those who trust in the Lord will rise up and stand firm" (Ps 20:7-8).

6. **The sixth strand is the power this grief has to pull us into deeper despair.** This is where we need the intervention of the prayer of spiritually mature people of God to break the bondage of despair in our souls. A few weeks ago I was steeped in the frustration of trying to rework this book. I was anxious, irritable, burdened, and discouraged. One day, Vivian was giving thanks for a meal when she prayed for God to strengthen my inner man. At that moment the Holy Spirit broke the strangling power of hopelessness in my wearied and troubled spirit and enabled me to move forward with fresh vigor and purpose.

7. **The seventh strand is the combined lack of three things: refuge, strength, and help that can be found in God and a loving community.** For various reasons, many of us lack the encouragement and support of a spiritually healthy and loving faith community, be it a local church and/or home group. Especially during times of trials and the Dark Night, we need one another to help us stand firm and press through (Heb 3:13; 10:24-25) and to remind us that, "God is our refuge and strength, an ever-present help in trouble" (Ps 46:1). If you do not have a church community, ask God to guide you to one.

Actions (for personal and group study):

1. Finish reading the gospel of John.

2. Memorize and give thanks for who God is to you in Psalm 46:1—your refuge, strength, and an ever-present help in trouble.

3. Start reading Isaiah chapters 40-66 and ask God to show you who He is and who you are to Him.

CHAPTER **10**

The Grief of Wondering If Any Good Is Going to Come

Testimony of Gordon MacDonald: "Most of us can trace back across the years of our lives and describe a mountain range of crises—some greater or taller than others. I have known the crises of watching my parents dissolve a twenty-five-year marriage, of almost flunking out of college because in my youthfulness I lacked the will to persevere in difficult times, of helplessly watching our two-year-old daughter come close to death (or potential brain damage) because she had mistaken whitened turpentine for milk in a cereal bowl. I remember the crises of severe financial stress, of a severe moment of personal despair that made me wonder if I was losing my mind, of a disappointment so bewildering that I found myself questioning if I knew how to hear God's voice at all ... But no crisis in my life has equaled a time several years ago when I engaged in a sequence of choices that eventuated in a total personal failure. It was a disruptive moment that featured betrayal, shame and humiliation, the apparent loss of all things (except my family and some incredibly faithful friends)."[49]

Paul's four word pictures to describe his DNX— "But we have this treasure in jars of clay to show that this all-surpassing power is from God and not from us. We are *hard pressed* on every side, but not crushed; *perplexed*, but not in despair; *persecuted*, but not abandoned; *struck down*, but not destroyed" (2 Cor 4:8-9; italics added).

1. Hard pressed on every side

This phrase echoes the familiar saying "between a rock and a hard place" with one additional element—falling boulders threatening to crush us and throw us off the cliff.

2. Perplexed

We are "perplexed" when things do not make sense to us. We are in turmoil and in conflict with God for His silence and lack of action. Strung out over an extended period of time, this prolonged agony easily sinks us into despair. How do people handle their despair? *How do you?*

3. Persecuted

We are "persecuted" when we are relentlessly pursued and harassed by something or someone. We feel that we are utterly forsaken and abandoned, helpless and defenseless.

---

49   Gordon MacDonald. *The Life God Blesses*. (Nashville: Thomas Nelson Inc. 1994), 65-66.

4. Struck down

We are "struck down" because of the blows to our body forcing us onto the ground. Our lives and all that define us and guarantee us a future are blown apart as if by explosives.

But wait! **Paul is not finished yet. The most amazing part of Paul's description has to do with the three-letter word "but,"** which appears 5 times in the three verses quoted. "We are hard pressed on every side, *but* not crushed; perplexed, *but* not in despair; persecuted, *but* not abandoned; struck down, *but not* destroyed" (2 Cor 4:8-9; italics added).

In my fourth year of university, a friend and I moved into an old and small trailer a few miles from campus. It was foolhardy of me to have signed up for an eight o'clock class, because I could not get up in time or run fast enough to make it. *What happened then?* I had a poor attendance record and could not keep up with the course work. One afternoon I was so discouraged that I decided to take a nap. Before I dozed off, I started to sing, "Nobody loves me. Everybody hates me. I am going to eat some worms—big, fat juicy worms." Then I had a dream (I think). In the dream I was looking down at the trailer I was living in. "What would make people take notice of me and this trailer?" I wondered. Then I was struck with a thought. "What happens if the government comes and fills this trailer with gold bars?" Can you imagine every nook and cranny of this old trailer stuffed with gold bars? The trailer may look the same on the outside, but its value has skyrocketed. Because of what is deposited on the inside, the trailer is now guaranteed special protection and care.

Using this dream God spoke to me about the word *"but"* in 2 Corinthians 4:7. *"But* we have this treasure in jars of clay to show that this all-surpassing power is from God and not from us." We all are like fragile, scarred, and easily broken clay pots. Like the old trailer, we may look the same as any other ordinary looking human being. But to God we are immeasurably priceless because of the treasure of Jesus Christ, who lives in us. We are the center of God's special attention and interest. We are His beloved. And it is because of His indwelling presence that we are able to rise above life's adverse circumstances, being "hard pressed ... , *but not* crushed; perplexed, *but not* in despair; persecuted, *but not* abandoned; struck down, *but not* destroyed" (2 Cor 4:8-9; italics added).

So, then, is there any good that can come from our DNX? Yes, there are at least seven benefits we can claim from our DNX.

First, Spiritual Benefits—There is no limit to what God is able to do in, through, and for us through our DNX. A few examples to affirm the promise, "No eye has seen, no ear has heard, no mind has conceived what God has prepared for those who love him" (1 Cor 2:9).

Perseverance, character and hope that does not disappoint - Romans 5:3-5;

Maturity and wisdom - James 1:4- 5;

Faith refined that is of greater worth than gold - 1 Peter 1:6-7;

Being restored and made strong, firm and steadfast - 1 Peter 5:10;

Sharing in His holiness and a harvest of righteousness and peace - Hebrews 12:10-11.

Second, Personal Benefit—There are four observable changes in us: from arrogance to acceptance; from bitterness to brokenness; from confidence in self to confidence in God, and from fighting God to trusting God.[50]

Third, Eternal Benefit—John Piper reminds us that "God has appointed our pain to be part of his powerful display of the glory of Christ"[51] so that "[m]any will see and fear and put their trust in the LORD" (Ps 40:3b). The power of our hope anchored in the Person and promises of God shines the brightest in the darkest hour.

Fourth, Relational Benefit—DNX helps us grow in sensitivity to our own and others' pain and suffering. When we experience God's truth and grace (Jn 1:14) we can extend them to others.

Fifth, Ministerial Benefit—DNX changes the way we do ministry. Here are some before and after comparisons.

"Before	After
happen to do ministry	follow God's leading in ministry
unaware of gifts	make ministry decisions based on gifting
happen upon a ministry role	make proactive choices for the appropriate ministry role
do ministry to meet own needs	ministering with God as the source
minister in own strength	minister by relying on God's strength
do faddish ministry	do purposeful ministry

50 Billheimer, ibid., *Don't Waste*, 75.
51 John Piper, *Filling up the Afflictions of Christ: The Cost of Bringing the Gospel to the Nations in the Lives of William Tyndale, Adoniram Judson, and John Paton.* (Wheaton: Crossway Books, 2009), 10.

small sphere of influence   usually a larger sphere of influence."[52]

Sixth, Spiritual Authority, an amazing by-product—Dr. J. Robert Clinton said, "All leaders face deep processing at some time in their lives. Many do so more than once. Deep processing refers to those activities that God uses to force a leader to seriously evaluate life and ministry. God uses such activities as isolation, conflict, and life crises (health or otherwise) to deepen a leader's relationship with God, to create a sense of utter dependence upon God, and to build foundational leadership character qualities in their life. From this kind of shaping activity, superintended by God, comes an important by-product: spiritual authority."[53]

Seventh, a new song and a new life message—David fell into a pit (DNX) and could not get out. He learned to "wait patiently" for the Lord and was given a new song and a new life message to share with others after his pit experience (Ps 40:1-3).

I believe the ultimate *good* God has for us in DNX is to mature and reap the blessings of knowledge, wisdom and understanding.

"**Blessed** is the man who finds wisdom, the man who gains understanding, for she is **more profitable** than silver and yields better returns than gold. She is **more precious** than rubies; nothing you desire can compare with her. **Long life** is in her right hand; in her left hand are **riches and honor**. Her ways are **pleasant ways**, and all her paths are **peace**. She is a **tree of life** to those who embrace her; those who lay hold of

52 Trebesch, *Isolation,* 54.
53 Ibid., v.

her will be **blessed**" (Prv 3:13-18).

Testimony by Phillip Keller of his Mother: "My mother, as a radiant bride of twenty-one years, and her handsome young husband Karl Wittich, had heard that cry. In response to the compelling conviction of God's Spirit they responded in positive action. Stepping out in unflinching faith they sailed for East Africa with another young man, Clarence Grothaus...

"Their first outpost was a disease-ridden area, inland hundreds of miles from the coast. They settled down to live among strange tribes people, speaking a strange language. It was decided that finding a fresh water supply was absolutely essential. So both men began to dig a well. It was a dreadful job in the tropical heat under an equatorial sun.

"Finally one evening a small seep of water began to spring from the stony bottom of the well. The three young people were almost delirious with delight. They had struck water! To celebrate they drew up a kettle full and made their first pot of tea.

"But there was death, not life, in that well. ... And within three days both young men were dead. The young lady lay writhing in a delirium of agony....

"There she was, half a world away from her family, her friends, her home. Alone among a strange people in a strange land, she was cut off from all human comfort and consolation. Stripped of her beloved; stripped of health; stripped of human support; she could find consolation only in Christ.

"Taken by porters to a distant railway station she was deposited in a dark room, certain that she would die there. Life was cheap in the African bush. Most human bodies were tossed outside at night to be consumed by hyenas. Fortunately, she was spared that death. Instead her rugged constitution helped her to recover, and she rallied from the very verge of the grave.

"Heart-broken and red-eyed with weeping, lonely and forlorn, she pled with God for release from her agony. She begged that she, too, might die. But His word to her was, 'Your work in Africa is not yet done.'

"So with incredible courage and indomitable determination she went back to the bush—back to her humble hut of mud and thatch—back to her beloved black neighbors who now were sure she had in very truth been raised from the dead.

"Almost immediately after this, the dreadful First World War of 1914-1918 erupted like a volcano on the world scene. The deadly outfall reached as far as East Africa's bush country. There German and British troops fought fierce skirmishes across the sun-blasted countryside. Men died in bloody battles; ... and all communication with the outside world was cut off.

"Apparently the only message ever to reach the young woman's family was a terse cable that merely stated 'Karl and Clarence dead. Marion recovering!'"[54]

In spite of all the hardships, Marion went back to the village

---

54   Phillip Keller, *Wonder O' the Wind* (London: Hodder and Stoughton Ltd, 1984), 23-25.

and became the bearer of Good News to many.

Actions (for personal and group study):

1. Is there anything undermining your confidence in God that you are struggling with?

2. Memorize and meditate on 2 Corinthians 12:9-10. List the promises of God in these verses. What do you have to do to make these promises effective in your life?

Part II
Thrive with the GPS CROWN Gifts

CHAPTER 11

Introduction: the GPS CROWN Gifts

Question: A weary missionary who came back to North America for a short and much needed furlough asked me, "How do you define Dark Night of the Soul Experience (DNX)? Is it just like depression?"

I answered her by saying, "St. John of the Cross used four words to describe DNX: terrible, horrible, awful, and bitter. As a result, DNX can trigger depression. I believe DNX is more than depression. It is a stripping away and reshaping process under the skillful and loving hand of God to make us into an instrument for His special purpose." I then repeated to her, in the following, the biblical concept of a branch-to-arrow word picture I wrote about in chapter 1 of this book.

A speaker was holding in her hand a branch full of leaves and fruits. As she was speaking she started to strip the leaves, the fruit, and the bark off the branch with a knife. After a few minutes we finally figured out what she was doing. She was making an arrow from the branch. She was stripping away all that adorned the branch—the leaves, the fruits, the bark, and the big, beautiful and fruitful tree it was attached to. If the branch could talk, it would be telling us how this painful process was taking away all that made the branch feel secure, significant, and purposeful in its existence. Meanwhile, the branch was clueless as to what was really going on and why the seemingly wonton destruction of its beauty was happening. Then the speaker shared Isaiah 49:2b: "He made me into a polished arrow and concealed me in his quiver."

The branch has every reason to doubt the love and wisdom of the arrow maker, because the process is truly painful and seems to be without rhyme or reason. After the stripping, the sanding, and polishing comes the fitting of the sharp tip and the feathers. Finally, the end is in sight. The branch has become an arrow but it may still think like a branch. Maybe it is expecting to be re-attached to the tree from where it first came. Then something completely insane happens.

Without explanation the archer puts the newly finished arrow into a deep, dark, smelly place called the quiver and leaves it there for an indefinite period of time.

Then, at some pre-appointed time, the arrow is taken out and fired across an unknown distance toward an unfamiliar landscape into a target designated by the master. Similar to the process of a branch becoming an arrow, our DNX, under the skillful, wise, and careful hand of our loving Father and Master, transforms us to fulfill His purpose. Like the arrow which feels the rushing wind as it flies through the air toward the target, we too can know the satisfying sense of fulfillment as we are deployed for His purpose and His glory.

"How do we survive, revive, and thrive in DNX?"

Most of us stumble along in our DNX by trial and error. The legendary basketball player Michael Jordan once said, "You can practice shooting eight hours a day, but if your technique is wrong, then all you become is very good at shooting the wrong way. Get the fundamentals down and the level of everything you do will rise."[55] Are there fundamentals for surviving, reviving, and thriving in DNX? GPS CROWN is the acronym for the eight fundamental gifts God has given us to be more than conquerors in the furnace of DNX. Each of the eight letters will be explained and explored in the following chapters. By way of introduction, here is a brief sketch of this eight-pronged GPS CROWN approach taken from John 20-21.

After the disciples experienced the riotous crowd and the cruel torture and crucifixion of Jesus, their hopes and dreams for a liberated Jewish nation were crushed. They cowered behind closed doors filled with fear, confusion, and doubts (Jn 20:19). Even the appearance of the resurrected Christ did not completely lift their dark clouds (Jn 20:1-9). How did the disciples change from being discouraged and desperate to bold apostles who later turned the world upside down (Acts 4:13)? The GPS CROWN pathway shows us how.

Jesus showed up (**G**—**G**od's presence) with the pronouncement of "peace be with you" (Jn 20:19, 21, 26). Later, when the disciples were fishing all night with nothing to show for it, Jesus showed up a third time on the shore and instructed them to lower the net again (Jn 21:4–6a). In spite of their weariness,

---

55   www.finestquotes.com/author_quotes-author-Michael%20Jordan-page-0.htm

the disciples chose to humbly obey and lower their net one more time. To their great surprise, they were not able to haul in the net because of the 153 large fish in it (Jn 21:6b, 11). Instead, they had to tow the net to shore (Jn 21:8). As they huddled over a breakfast of bread and fish prepared by Jesus on a fire of burning coals, the disciples knew without any doubt that they were in the presence of their resurrected Lord (Jn 21:12).

Having displayed the attitude of a learner, the disciples had the privilege of witnessing the miraculous work of God at sea and were restored again into the circle of fellowship with their Master. They were re-commissioned again for His purpose (P) to "Follow me ... and I will make you fishers of men" (Mt 4:19). Peter, John, and other disciples were together in God's ordained, nurturing setting (S) to experience Christ's presence and ministry among them. In choosing (C) to obey Jesus's simple instruction to lower their net again, the disciples were able to experience God's wonderful re-creation (R) of their whole person and outlook on their future.

During His personal encounter with Peter after breakfast, Jesus asked Peter three times, "Simon, son of John, do you truly love me?" (Jn 21:15-17). Peter must have been overwhelmed by the memory of his three denials and the ready acceptance and forgiveness of Christ by being restored again to "feed His sheep" (Jn 21:15-17). In the same way, after Peter's and the other disciples' DNX, Jesus also prepares each of us with our God-given gifts, talents, experiences, and skills (**O will be explained in chapter 17**) for His purposes as wounded healers (W) to the wounded in this world. Then Jesus said something "to indicate the kind of death by which Peter would glorify God" (Jn 21:19). Peter turned and looked behind at his friend

John and asked, "Lord, what about him?" Jesus answered, "What is that to you?" In other words, "It is none of your business (**N**), Peter. Your responsibility is to follow me."

Testimony of John & Vivian Moy

John—"In 1968 I was learning to be Christ's disciple and disciple-maker with The Navigators on my college campus. For various personal reasons I decided not to be involved in the dating scene. Then one summer at a conference I met Vivian. We ended up dating, seriously, long distance. At the end of that school year I was challenged by Dave, a member of the local Navigator staff, to break up with Vivian for the purpose of deepening my walk with God and growing in skill and maturity in a disciple-making ministry. Dave shared three verses with me: 1. 'Hope deferred makes the heart sick, but a longing fulfilled is a tree of life' (Prv 13:12). 2. 'So he gave them what they asked for, but sent a wasting disease upon them' (Ps 106:15). 3. 'For the revelation awaits an appointed time; it speaks of the end and will not prove false. Though it linger, wait for it; it will certainly come and will not delay' (Hb 2:3).

"Unknown to me at the time, my maturity in Christ was hindered by the unresolved grief and anger from my broken-home upbringing. They were like open wounds that refused to be healed. From this grew a secret demand that became a stronghold, to have a wife and my own family. To help me mature, God had to dismantle the stronghold, bring me to the end of my will and power, and find His sufficiency for my deepest thirsts and needs. I had to take a step of faith and obedience to believe in Him who truly 'rewards those who earnestly seek Him' (Heb 11:6). I was wresting with the implications of this life changing decision while I attended a Navigators' summer training camp in Nebraska.

"One Sunday afternoon I was walking around a big lake agonizing before God. I did not have the desire, power, or will to even want to break up with Vivian. I ended up kneeling behind a big rock crying out to the Lord for not having what it takes to obey Him. Then I heard singing from heaven. It was in English. The music was beautiful. In my daze and agony I looked for this wonder. Then I realized the singing was not from that far up. It was coming from a loudspeaker on a telephone pole near the big rock. I heard the words again and again, 'Trust and obey for there is no other way to be happy in Jesus but to trust and obey.' As I yielded my will to obey, the Lord's power and sufficient grace enabled me to have the will and power to embrace His will to break up with Vivian. The only request I asked of God was to prepare Vivian's heart to receive the 'Dear John' letter from 'Dear John.'"

Vivian—"My father died when I was two. I grew up with my mother and a younger sister. In spite of a loving home and a supportive extended family network, I grew up not liking or valuing myself. I was an extreme introvert and ill at ease in social gatherings. I often became suspicious of others' motives when they paid me complements or any attention because I considered myself undeserving and unworthy of their gestures. Deep down I yearned to love and be loved but was paralyzed by self-doubt and a destructive sense of unworthiness.

"Even after I put my faith in Jesus for my salvation, I continued to struggle with the sense of 'never good enough' for anything or anyone, including the God who saved me. Even though

I had a strong desire to please God, the Christian life was a daily grind of 'dos and don'ts,' 'should,' 'have to,' and 'or else.' I assumed the Christian life was supposed to be joyless and dull but a necessary part of living. Then I met John at a Chinese Christian conference one summer. Through him I met fellow believers who exhibited a rare (to me then) combination of a great zest for life and a deep commitment to God.

"I was jealous! I so wanted to be like them but was secretly afraid to find out how. Being kept from attending the same session of the training camp as John, I opted for the second session out of sheer determination to prove to myself that I could do it. I was so surprised that I actually loved every minute of being at camp.

"Sleeping in a room with five other strangers in two triple-bunk beds did not faze me at all. Working as a team of cook's helpers in the kitchen was fun. Getting up in the dark to do calisthenics was a breeze. I engrossed myself in doing Bible study and joining in daily worship. I began to feel alive inside, excited that I was part of something big and significant beyond myself. Life was good. *How did I miss all of this before?*

"One Saturday morning, during time alone with God, I read through Psalm 139. My life was turned upside down when I re-discovered God's unconditional love for me. I stood totally accepted by God because of Christ's righteousness imputed to me. I was highly valued because of the price paid for my purchase from slavery to sin and death. Living the Christian life could no more be dependent on the sheer determination of my bankrupt will and strength. It could now be a joyous possibility of cooperating with God, who promised to work in me, like riding the waves and being carried along toward the shore. The impact of this revelation was so forceful that I felt like being born again a second time. I came away with an insatiable thirst to know God and His Word. I was willing to do anything.

"This exchange with God prepared me to receive the 'Dear John' letter from 'dear John' the very next day after the Sunday morning message on Luke 14:26-27. (The miracle here is that there is no mail delivery on Sunday.) As a result, to agree to break up with John came easier than I expected. Tears did not come until much later, but with no regrets. I needed time to deepen my walk with God and mature emotionally. This DNX lasted three years before God saw fit to bring us back together.

"We just celebrated our 42nd anniversary. I truly believe that without those years apart to mature, our marriage would not have survived the rigors of life and ministry. Winter is a necessary season for us to be nourished and refreshed before the season of growth."

Actions (for personal and group study):

1. What have you learned about God, yourself, and others in this chapter?

2. List and explain three take-aways or warnings for yourself.

3. Is there one issue God keeps bringing up in your life that you need to pray about and deal with? Seek godly and biblical counsel before you act or react.

CHAPTER **12**

The Gift of God's Presence (G)

Vivian—"Sitting in front of me was a group of mature adults who had been Christians for 10 plus years and were actively involved in all aspects of a thriving church life. Most were lay leaders who busied themselves running and promoting a variety of programs for their respective ministries. Now they were telling me what they really thought about the Christian life, that it was all a pipe dream, out of reach and impossible to live out. I was shocked! No wonder they were tired and weary, running out of energy and ideas to keep programs going and people interested. There was no joy in what they were doing. They were desperate to get off the merry-go-round and let someone else take over. What would happen if, in the middle of their joyless and tiring service, they were blindsided by a DNX? Is it any wonder that 90% of Christians never move past this bitter and painful experience and remain stuck in disillusion about God and the Christian life? We see many Christians living like paupers instead of living like princes and princesses of the resurrected Christ."

The first precious gift from God to survive, revive, and thrive in DNX is God's presence (G), which is the gift of God HIMSELF with all His love and resources. Many of us often fail to enter into His presence in DNX because our hearts are churning like a boiling pot. I once asked a friend who lost her child to suicide, "Is it possible to be in the presence of God with peace... and pain at the same time?" Without hesitation she emphatically replied, "YES! YES! YES!"

Question: how to deal with the problem of a churning heart?

Our churning heart is like a boiling pot that demands our immediate attention. If ignored, the consequences can be dangerous, scary, and irreparable. Years ago, one Sunday after church, Vivian suddenly exclaimed, "Oh no, I forgot to turn off the stove with tonight's stew." Right away we all got into the car and rushed home. When we opened the front door, the house was full of thick black smoke from the burnt pieces in the pot. We quickly turned off the stove, which, thankfully, was set on low. The very hot pot was carefully moved to the deck outside. Even with all the windows and doors opened and the exhaust fan on full blast, it was quite some time before the smoke was cleared and the smell dissipated.

The black and crusty parts that stuck to the bottom of the pot took the longest time and hardest work to clean. Several times Vivian threatened to just throw it away. In the same way, if we ignore the call for action, the churning may turn into a real threat. Sooner or later, what is boiling and churning inside will cause damage within us and impair relationships. It may sweep a person to the dark side, into a dark place where they may plan some very dark deeds.

There are four causes that lead to churning in our hearts. Many of these issues are normal human experiences and concerns that easily get ignored and buried under the clamor of everyday living. DNX is God's way to help us examine, address, identify, and resolve the cause(s) of our churning heart so that we may experience His presence more and more fully and deeply.

- Struggles of the heart—Ordinary everyday seemingly inconsequential struggles, doubts, questions, and concerns are magnified and brought to sharper focus during DNX. Instead of being muffled by the demands of everyday life, they are now screaming for attention and refusing to be ignored.

- Pains of the heart—Unresolved grief and regrets from losses that linger and fester.

- Barriers of the heart— Deep-seated and entrenched strongholds that we stubbornly defend, refusing to let the light of God's Word shine in. "Arguments and every lofty opinion [that] is raised against the knowledge of God" (2 Cor 10:5, ESV).

- Sores of the heart—Sore spots and hurting areas of our life that have not been healed properly. Like a physical wound, we react violently whenever someone brings up the occasion or the person responsible for our hurt.

How do we encourage or come alongside those whose hearts are churning?

For me, to encourage means to appreciate, to affirm, and to

acknowledge. People with churning hearts do not need to be told what to do or to be preached at or persuaded to do more. They are like the boiling pot: pressure needs to be released, heat turned off, and the house cleaned with help. A much better and affirming way to help is to ask the right questions at the right time, to be a good listener, and to offer practical solutions to release the pressure with much prayer, patience, and creativity.

In a conversation with a seasoned missionary couple in DNX, I shared with them the simple GAS model on emotions, which stands for grief, guilt, anger, anxiety, stress, and shame. I then asked, "What is foremost in your thoughts these days? Which of these emotions is constantly boiling up in you?" The sharing that followed proved to be surprisingly revealing, even to themselves and to each other. As they shared, they were clarifying the tangled web of emotions and thoughts in their own souls. They were acknowledging out loud what was on their hearts and minds. This release of pressure then helps them take baby steps forward in their DNX.

Presence of God for life's challenges—examples from Scriptures:

1. Facing an impossible task—God revealed Himself to **Moses** as "I AM", the "I AM WHO I AM" who would be **with him** when he led God's people of millions out of slavery in Egypt into the Promised Land of Canaan (Ex 3:12-14).

2. Famine in a foreign and hostile land—**Isaac** and his band were living as strangers in a hostile, foreign land

when famine struck. God's instruction to Isaac was, "Stay in this land for a while, and I will be **with you** and will bless you" (Gn 26:3, 13, 26-28).

3. After a personal failure—After **Jacob** cheated his elder brother out of his blessing, he fled to his ancestral land. Jacob was surprised when God spoke to him, "I am **with you** and will watch over you wherever you go, and I will bring you back to this land. I will not leave you until I have done what I have promised you" (Gn 28:15; cf., 31:42).

4. Facing betrayal and slavery--**Joseph** was sold by his brothers as a slave to Egypt. He remained faithful to God and "the Lord was **with him** and ... gave him success in everything he did" (Gn 39:2-6, 20-23). Joseph spent a total of 13 years as a slave and a prisoner on false charges before he became second only to Pharaoh and saved his family from famine.

5. Facing the bitterness and scoffing of barrenness— **Hannah** never knew the impact of her prayer when she was agonizing over the pain of barrenness and the cruel scoffing from "the other wife" year after year. She pleaded with God for a son in her deep distress and promised to give him back to the Lord "all the days of his life" (1 Sm 1:11). Hannah's request was granted and she kept her promise. In turn "[t]he LORD was **with Samuel** as he grew up, and He let none of his words fall to the ground" (1 Sm 3:19). In God's big picture, Samuel would turn the Israelites back to God and usher in Jesus the Christ, the Savior of the world.

6. Facing moral failures, murder and powerful enemies—
   In his lifetime **David** faced many powerful enemies
   but "[i]n everything he did he had great success, because the LORD was **with him**" (1Sm 18:14). Even
   in his many glaring personal failures and sins, David
   was restored into God's presence when he humbly re-
   pented and returned to his God.

7. Facing a mammoth task— **Solomon** was chosen for
   the mammoth task of building the temple of God. His
   father, David, admonished him, "Be strong and cou-
   rageous, and do the work. Do not be afraid or discouraged, for the LORD God, my God, is **with you**.
   He will not fail you or forsake you until all the work
   for the service of the temple of the LORD is finished"
   (1Chr 28:20).

8. Facing the need of the world for salvation—The birth
   of Jesus was prophesized as one who would be called
   "Emmanuel—which means 'God **with us**' " (Mt 1:23).
   Jesus appointed the twelve as apostles so that "they
   might be **with him**" (Mk 3:14). To prepare His disci-
   ples for His impending absence, Jesus promised the
   coming of the Holy Spirit to be **with them** and in them
   (Jn 14:16-17). Before returning to the Father, Jesus
   gave His last command with a promise, "And surely
   I am **with you** always, to the very end of the age"
   (Mt 28:20). During the early days of His Church, "The
   Lord's hand was **with them**, and a great number of
   people believed and turned to the Lord" (Acts 11:21).
   At the end of the ages, the dwelling of God will be
   with men, "and He will live **with them**" (Rv 21:3).

Experiencing the reality of His presence in our lives depends on our choosing to abide in HIM by His power. "**The LORD is with you when you are with him**. If you seek him, he will be found by you" (2 Chr 15:2).

How do we enter into His presence? In Ephesians 1:17-21 Paul teaches us how to daily recall our *identity* and *inheritance* in Christ that enables us to access divine resources to face life challenges in DNX. It is the four-part SHIP prayer.

1. **S** (1:17): "God may fill you with the **Spirit of wisdom and revelation**, so that you may know Him better." Start each day asking for the filling of His Spirit of wisdom and revelation for the purpose of knowing Jesus better through prayer, the Word of God, and practical obedience. We also need the Spirit of wisdom and revelation to discern pitfalls and potholes in DNX and our physical, mental, emotional, and spiritual states and needs.

2. **H** (1:18): "[T]he eyes of your heart may be enlightened in order that you may know the hope to which he has called you," "a **living hope**" (1 Pt 1:3, emphasis mine) for the present and beyond in eternity. This living hope sustains us in our trials and suffering. It gives value to all that we do in His name (1 Cor 15:58). This hope helps us make choices with eternal value in mind, knowing that one day we will give an account for what we do and how we live (2 Cor 5:10). It also serves as an anchor for our life—"We have this hope as an anchor for the soul, firm and secure" (Heb 6:19). Without the anchor of hope, we will not find rest but

will continually drift and be tossed about by the ups and downs of life's circumstances.

3. **I** (1:18): "[T]he riches of his glorious **inheritance** in the saints." What is our glorious inheritance? Many of them are stated in Ephesians chapter one relating to the phrase *in Christ.* Here is one of them in verse 3—"every spiritual blessing" that we need for life has been given to us **in** Christ. There are at least 25 items of inheritance in the chapter. See how many you can find and give thanks to God for each of them. It will change your life.

4. **P** (1:19-21): "His incomparably great **power** for us who believe. That power is like the working of his mighty strength, which he exerted in Christ when he raised him from the dead and seated him at his right hand in the heavenly realms, far above all rule and authority, power and dominion, and every title that can be given, not only in the present age but also in the one to come." Do you know the power and authority the Holy Spirit fills you with daily is the same that raised Jesus from the dead? Paul wrote in Philippians 4:13, "I can do everything through him who gives me strength." The same power and strength is yours also in Christ. Do you know it?

Himself

Once it was the blessing, Now it is the Lord;
Once it was the feeling, Now it is His Word;
Once His gift I wanted, Now, the Giver own;

Once I sought for healing, Now Himself alone.
All in all forever, Only Christ I'll sing.
Everything in Christ, and Christ is everything.[56]

Actions (for personal and group study):

1. Identify the issues of your churning heart on a piece of paper. Ask God for wisdom (Jas 1:5) and "safe people" to help you face these challenges in your life. Remember the statement, "Inch by inch is a cinch."

2. Read, memorize, reflect, and pray the *SHIP* prayer into your heart and daily life. Concentrate on what God has given you "in Christ," not on what you don't have or have lost. Secondly, accept the present for what it is, the past for what it was, and the future for what it will be, depending on what we choose to be and do in Christ daily.

---

56 First verse of the hymn *Once It Was the Blessing* by A. B. Simpson, 1843-1919. www.hymnal.net/hymn.php/h/513#ixzz2kShPuxyV.

CHAPTER 13

The Gift of God's Purpose and Process in a Person (P)

A young mom came to me for counseling. Her life was falling apart. She was stuck in a bad marriage and she was afraid for the safety of her children. Her husband was living in depression and nightly isolation in his study. As her story unfolded, I realized that she was the "other woman" for whom the young husband had left his wife and children. Now, a few years later, both of them were living with major GAS—guilt, grief, anger, anxiety, snare, stress, and shame. She asked me, "Is there hope for me and my children?"

Another woman confessed to us that for 40 years she was angry at God for taking away her favorite sibling through sickness. She blamed her loss and pain on the surviving spouse, who had patiently endured the abuse with the love of Christ. Now, this woman felt guilty and ashamed. Could she be set free?

A friend said, "I have been hiding a hurt that happened 35 years ago. It is still weeping pus."

How do we know we are still struggling with DNX?

These are some common struggles I have observed in people I know in their DNX:

- We try running away from our heart pains with many good activities or lack of activities without engaging and embracing our pain and grief.

- We keep looking at "want ads" for an immediate escape from our unpleasant situation.

- We allow bitterness and unforgiveness to remain in our hearts.

- We use addictive means to numb and dumb the pain.

- We learn to fix the blame but not fix (and face) the problem.

- We beat ourselves up with derogatory and accusatory thoughts.

- We cannot stop repeating to others how we were maligned and mistreated.

- We are invaded by sleepless nights filled with revengeful and bitter thoughts.

- We cannot stop complaining, comparing, and competing with others in our own mind.

- We are not able to enter into God's Promised Land

of rest because of our *URGE*: **u**nwilling to do what God wants, **r**ebellion against God's specific teaching, **g**rumbling against others and thinking God is **e**vil for putting us in our situation (Dt 1:26-27).

- We cannot fight off the continuous doubt about God's love for us.

- We are stuck in our painful experience of life and cannot move forward.

The mother of a missing man said, "We are torn apart. The pain is unimaginable. Every day is more than awful." (*Langley Times*, March 25, 2009, 1)

In the book *Spiritual Rhythm,* author Mark Buchanan describes DNX as "the heart's winter"—a season bankrupt of pleasure and meaning. Buchanan states that our theology and our reality become irreconcilable in "winter" when God is nowhere to be found, when we experience "a terrible, terrifying aloneness" with only darkness as our closest companion. Winter is not a time for sowing, but more like death. But winter does have its purpose. It is a time for pruning and more pruning, for waiting and more waiting. Spring will come only after winter. Like a grain of wheat in the ground, new life emerges only after death.

People in DNX need: Safe people and a safe place to work through their pain and process their emotions without pressure to perform; a renewed sense of self-worth (Chapter 17); a renewed purpose in life (this chapter); and a pathway to restoration and renewal (Part II of the book).

The second precious gift for DNX is the gift of God's purpose and process in a person. I was shocked and surprised when I read God's reference to King David as "a man after His heart" (Acts 13:22) and that "David had served God's purpose in his own generation" (Acts 13:36). How could this be? Along with all the great acts of bravery and conquest, David was also a murderer, a weak father, and an adulterous and prideful king who had done harm to his own family and the people he governed. And yet, in God's evaluation, David was said to have served God's purpose in his own generation and was a man after God's heart. There is something radically different about God's evaluation of people that is totally beyond our grasp.

Nonetheless, from David's life we can be sure of one thing: God has a purpose for each of us to fulfill in our generation. Because we have the precious gift of God's presence in us, our life is not meaningless or a matter of fate. Ephesians 2:10 speaks of us as "God's workmanship created in Christ Jesus to do good works, which God prepared in advance for us to do." We may not understand all that He is doing as we go through the process (Prv 20:24), but we will eventually come to taste and see the purpose and the goodness of God (Jer 29:11).

Purpose in defining success

Many of us define success in terms of performance, position, power, possession, and popularity. In the same way, Jesus also was tempted (Lk 4:1-12). But Jesus overcame because He defined success according to God's purpose for which He was sent into the world—to do only the work the Father gave Him to do (Jn 5:19, 36). After only three short years of public ministry and on the eve of His impending death, Jesus was able to declare to the Father, "I have brought you glory on earth by completing the work you gave me to do" (Jn 17:4), even death on the cross. In the Old Testament, the life of Joseph, Daniel, and his three friends also demonstrated to us what true success is when they chose God and His plan in their DNX, even though God's purpose was still a mystery to them at the time.

At the end of my life, by God's grace, I too want to be able to say with the apostle Paul, "I have fought the good fight, I have finished the race, I have kept the faith" (2 Ti 4:7). I long to hear the Master's words to me, "Well done, good and faithful servant" (Mt 25:21)! What about you? How would you define or redefine success for your life?

What do we do in DNX? Most of us make it our aim to find a way out and solve our immediate challenges. St. John of the Cross's answer to the dilemma is intuitively contrary to ours. He said, "The way in which they are to conduct themselves in this night [DNX]…is not to devote themselves to reasoning and meditation, since this is not the time for it, but to allow the soul to remain in peace and quietness …"[57] For "a heart at peace gives life to the body" (Prv 14:30a), and "in quietness and trust is your strength" (Is 30:15). So "be still and know that I am God" (Ps 46:10).

How do we keep still, and be at peace and quiet? Two words— **God's sovereignty**. It is a theological term referring to the eternal God as the creator, ruler, and controller of all things, whose plans and purposes cannot be thwarted or frustrated (Is 14:27). It implies God's total freedom to do whatever is in accordance

---

57   Pratney, Thomas *Factor,* 184.

with His pleasure and will (Ps 115:3, Eph 1:11). God said, "I am the Lord, and there is no other; ... I form the light and create darkness, I bring prosperity and create disaster; I, the Lord, do all these things" (Is 45:5, 7).

In Acts 17:22-28 Paul proclaimed to an audience who worshipped "an unknown God" that God is the One "who made the world and everything in it. [He] is the Lord of heaven and earth ... He determined the times set for them [mankind] and the exact places where they should live. ... 'For in him we live and move and have our being.'" We can rest assured that God can be trusted with every single aspect of our life. We can stand on the knowledge that He is able to provide a way for us, as He did for King David, to reengage His good purpose for our life.

When I graduated from university and was on my way to be drafted into military service, Ken, a Navigator staff member, said to me, "John, never stop confessing." I guess he saw the road of reality for me. **King David found himself entangled in a mess of his own doings** (2 Sm 11). He committed adultery with Bathsheba when he should have been out with his troops. To extricate himself from his shameful secret, he had Bathsheba's husband killed and refused to repent until he was confronted by Nathan, the prophet. In Psalm 32 there are four steps David took that brought about his eventual restoration to God and His purpose. These steps can be summarized by the acronym "ACTS":

1. **I acknowledge my aches (A).** "When I kept silent, my bones wasted away through my groaning all day long. For day and night your hand was heavy upon me; my

strength was sapped as in the heat of summer" (Ps 32:3-4). David ached in silence until he finally owned up to his sins and chose not to cover up. "Then I ac-knowledged my sin to you and did not cover up my iniquity" (32:5).

2. **I confess (C).** David came clean and said, "I will con-fess my transgressions to the LORD" (32:5). David ac-knowledged that ultimately his sins were against God and that only God could forgive him. Therefore, in confessing to God in agreement with God's Word on his sins, David sought and received forgiveness from God (32:5).

3. **I trust (T).** As David experienced God's forgive-ness and cleansing, the reality of the mess he was in overwhelmed him. Is God able to help him unravel the ugly aftermath of his actions? God understands David's predicaments as well as ours and He gives us these assurances:

God, my problems are like a flood: "Therefore let ev-eryone who is godly pray to you while you may be found; surely when the mighty waters rise, they will not reach him" (32:6).

God, I need a place to hide: "You are my hiding place; you will protect me from trouble and surround me with songs of deliverance" (32:7).

God, I do not know what to do: "I will instruct you and teach you in the way you should go; I will counsel you and watch over you. Do not be like the horse or the mule, which have no understanding but must be controlled by bit and bridle or they will not come to you" (32: 8-9). God promises to instruct and lead us in the best path for us with His principles to live by. God will also help us step by step to practice these principles as we walk in His path.

God, I need your presence and your peace: "Many are the woes of the wicked, but the LORD's unfailing love surrounds the man who trusts in him" (32:10).

God, I failed again and again. Are you also going to leave me? God promises to surround us with his unfailing and steadfast love (32:10). **He would not leave us or forsake us.**

4. **I set (S).** Like David, we set our heart to acknowledge and give thanks for God's forgiveness and abundant grace that restore us to Him. "Blessed is he whose transgressions are forgiven, whose sins are covered" (32:1). "Blessed is the man whose sin the LORD does not count against him and in whose spirit is no deceit" (32:2).

And the **God** of all **grace** *(the source and giver of all and every kind of grace that sustains our faith)*, who called you to his eternal **glory** in Christ *(His presence, our calling, and destiny in Him)*, after you have suffered *(grief)* a little while, will himself *(guarantee to)* restore you and make you strong, firm and steadfast" (1 Pt 5:10 italics added).

Actions (for personal and group study):

1. Reflect and claim I Peter 5:10 as God's promise to you. What have you gleaned from this verse?

2. Read and reflect on the ACTS prayer and its application to your life. Don't stop confessing and entrusting yourself to God and walking in His presence and purpose.

3. Memorize and claim Hebrews 11:6, "And without faith it is impossible to please God, because anyone who comes to him must believe that he exists and that he rewards those who earnestly seek him."

4. Ask God to teach and demonstrate His sovereign rule and care for you this week.

CHAPTER 14

The Gift of God's Ordained Setting (S)

Philip Yancey: "People, who are suffering, whether from physical or psychological pain, often feel an oppressive sense of aloneness. They feel abandoned, by God and also by others, because they must bear the pain alone and no one else quite understands. Loneliness increases the fear, which in turn increases the pain, and downward the spiral goes."[58]

What do we need to walk through the DNX? We need safe people and a safe place of refuge to walk and work through our DNX without the pressure of an agenda.

Have you heard or said:

- "I believe in God but don't like the church."

- "I don't need to go to church to worship God. I can very well do that in the privacy of my own home with the television on."

---

58   Yancey, *Hurts,* 173.

- "I don't need other people in my life. Just God and I are enough."

- "I am sure I can handle the Dark Night if I just have enough faith in God."

We all are hardwired for relationship in community by divine design in creation (Gn 1:26-27; 2:18). No wonder solitary confinement is considered one of the cruelest forms of punishment. In God's redemptive plan, through faith and trust in Jesus Christ, we become brothers and sisters in the Family of God and members of the Body of Christ. Not only is God a "father to the fatherless, a defender of widows," He also "sets the lonely in families" (Ps 68:5-6). Charles Colson is convinced that "if we don't grasp *the intrinsically corporate nature of Christianity* embodied in the church, we are missing the very heart of Jesus' plan."[59] We in the western world are particularly vulnerable to this pitfall because our modern western culture is obsessively individualistic.[60]

What saddens me most is the reality that many Christian leaders, pastors, and missionaries cannot find safe people with whom they can be vulnerable and address their own pain and struggles. Some of us are hesitant to reach out for help in our DNX because of past hurtful experiences like the ones I quoted in chapter 2 from Edith Schaeffer:

"Do people swarm around you when you have gone through a tragedy of some sort and nearly destroy you with the kind

---

59   Charles Colson with Ellen Santilli Vaughn, *The Body: Being Light in Darkness* (Dallas: Word Publishing, 1992), 277.
60   Ibid., 276.

of 'comfort' which Job's comforters threw at him? 'There must be something wrong with your prayer life.' Or 'God must be pointing to a terrible sin in your life. You'd better search your heart.' Or 'I am sure that if you had more faith your child would be healed.' Or 'I know it will all turn out right. If you let Jesus lead you, you won't have difficulties like this anymore.' Or 'What you need is a real "experience." Then you won't have any more problems; every day will be filled with perfect joy.' Every sentence of such 'comfort' comes out as a criticism and a comparison."[61]

Who are the safe people? Dr. Henry Cloud and Dr. John Townsend have much to say about this topic in their book, *Safe People: How to Find Relationships That Are Good for You and Avoid Those That Aren't.* The following is a brief summary of their answers to the question: Safe people are people with the ability to connect with us in ways that we know they are present with us. Safe people unconditionally love and accept us just as we are. This is grace. We do not need to fear being shamed or condemned. Safe people are those who are real and honest about our faults, who walk in truth themselves, and who are committed to speaking the truth to us in love for our good.

Job and his friends

It is commendable that Job's three friends cared enough about their friend's suffering to organize a visit to comfort and show their sympathy, as seen in Job 2:11: "When they saw [Job] from a distance, they could hardly recognize him; they began to weep aloud, and they tore their robes and sprinkled dust on

---

61   Schaeffer, *Affliction*, 31.

their heads. Then they sat on the ground with [Job] for seven days and seven nights. No one said a word to [Job], because they saw how great his suffering was."

Job's three friends are demonstrating in a powerful and vivid way their ability to connect with Job in his terrible suffering. Their ministry is a life-giving ministry of presence. In chapter 12, I speak of the gift of God Himself, His presence with us. Here, it is the gift of oneself to another, especially in dark and painful times. So far, so good. But then "Job opened his mouth and cursed the day of his birth" (Jb 3:1).

Till now, Job has shown great restraint in not sinning in what he said or in charging God with wrongdoing (Jb 1:22; 2:10b). However, a powerful storm of thought and emotion is churning inside that needs an outlet and needs to be validated. After seven days and nights of his friends' presence, Job may have considered it finally safe to let loose the torrent that has been building up in his heart and mind. Regrettably, it is at this point that Job's friends fail him as safe people. As a matter of fact, they shame and condemn Job for causing his own suffering and do not speak the truth about God to Job. God bears witness to this when He says to one of Job's friends afterward, "I am angry with you and your two friends, because you have not spoken of me what is right" (Jb 42:7).

Our need for safe people in community becomes critical in DNX. Being connected to safe people "draws us closer to God, draws us closer to others and helps us become the real person God created us to be."[62]

---

62   Ibid., 143.

Why do we need safe people in DNX?

1. **To accept my DNX**—Acceptance to me means:

    - "It was the way it was." (I need to stop fighting what happened and move on with my life.)

    - "It is the way it is." (I need to accept that *what is* is *what is*.)

    - If I do not accept my life as it is, the rest of my life will be like driving a car with my eyes fixed on the rearview mirror. Sooner or later, I will have an accident, or worse.

    - I need to accept *what is now* as the new normal of my life. I may not understand or like it, yet this is all I have to work with and I need to give thanks for what is.

    - I need to let go of my demands and expectations of God, others, and myself.

    - I need to forgive those who hurt me as well as those who saw what happened and did nothing about it.

    - I need to acknowledge, confess, trust, and set (ACTS) my eyes on God again (Ps 32).

    - I need to trust and obey God again with His presence and His power, right here and right now, and leave others, circumstances, consequences, and the future to God.

- I need to be humble and not grumble or else I will crumble.

- I need to stay connected to safe people and God's healing community for renewal, restoration, and spiritual maturity.

- I need practical means, helps, and advice as life goes on.

2. **To practice humility**—accepting God's sovereignty in the midst of evil and bad personal choices. Humility means to bow down and submit ourselves to God with a **heart attitude of poverty, purity, and privilege.** "Blessed are the poor [i.e., abject **poverty**] in spirit, for theirs is the kingdom of heaven" (Mt 5:3). This heart attitude comes from our personal and painful experiences through which we recognize that we are at the end of our power, wisdom, cleverness, and resources. We are bankrupt and destitute! This is the scariest and most feared experience for all of us. We try repeatedly to fight it, avoid it, deny it, and blame others and the system for it. We loathe having our lives turned upside down with nothing to hold on to. We are mad at God for having our desires frustrated. We are in turmoil because our well-rehearsed answers from the Bible to life's problems are shattered and appear to contradict reality. What we believe about God becomes a mockery to us. We are afraid to acknowledge our state of being emotionally and spiritually bankrupt for fear that we might be stuck in it for good. We put on a mask. We isolate ourselves from fellowship and sink

deeper into our dark side in the dark place. The sure way out of this vicious cycle is to have safe people extend unconditional love and acceptance to us without fear of being shamed or condemned. Admitting that we have struggles and needs in a safe relationship opens the door to freedom and life.

In the midst of our poverty, God also works to purify us, giving us the **privilege** and ability to see and hear God at work in our lives and DNX. "Blessed are the **pure** in heart, for they will see God" (Mt 5:8).

Oswald Chambers observed, "After every time of darkness there comes a mixture of **delight** and **humiliation** (if there is delight only, I question whether we have heard God at all), delight in hearing God speak, but chiefly humiliation—What a long time I was in hearing that! How slow I have been in understanding that! ...Now He gives you the gift of humiliation which brings the softness of heart that will always listen to God *now*."[63]

3. **To cooperate with God**—In acknowledging our poverty in spirit and the inability in ourselves to submit and obey God, we have the promise that God is the One "who works in [us] **to *will* and to *act* according to his good purpose**" (Phil 2:13, emphasis added). It is easy to forget this precious assurance when we are tossed here and there in our Dark Night. Safe people help us regain our sightline on God and stop our striving. Instead, we can rest and cooperate with God's

---

63   Oswald Chambers. "February 14ᵗʰ: The Discipline of Heeding" in *My Utmost for His Highest: Selections for the Year* (New York: Dodd, Mead & Company, 1952), 45.

power, which motivates and empowers us to fulfill His good purpose and plan. In trust and obedience, we work out what God is working in us.

I was sitting with a group of eager and committed Christian workers who were discussing some very ambitious plans to reach the world for Jesus Christ. After about half an hour of talking and dining together, I threw out a question that shocked them. I told them how much I appreciated their heart for God and then asked, "What will happen when, for whatever reasons (maybe a heartbreak, a loss, a DNX, etc.), you come to the place in your life when your drive and heart for everything of God dries up?" Stares and silence! I then had the privilege of sharing the truth of God's promise here in Philippians. This twin truth is the master key to running the race God sets for each of us, and finishing well. "Even youths grow tired and weary, and young men stumble and fall; but those who hope in the Lord will renew their strength. ... [T]hey will run and not grow weary, they will walk and not be faint" (Is 40:30-31).

4. **To process grief**—since loss and grief are an integral part of DNX, we need understanding and support from others to walk through our grief. People who have experienced trauma and death in their lives tell us how critical community is to their survival and healing, not just at the point of crisis but even more so afterward. We need a friend "who loves at all times" and a brother or sister "born for adversity" (Prv 17:17). They are the safe people who are present with us in our grief and speak to us truth that inspires hope for the future.

Here are the **five stages of grief** identified by Kubler-Ross[64]:

1. **Denial** (This isn't *happening* to me!)

2. **Anger** (Why is this happening to *me*?)

3. **Bargaining** (I promise I'll be a better person *if...*)

4. **Depression** (I don't *care* anymore)

5. **Acceptance** (*I'm ready* for whatever comes)

"If you want to go fast, go alone. If you want to go far, go together."–Ancient African proverb

Actions (for personal and group study):

1. The Christian life is a marathon to be run individually in community. DNX is a time when we are most prone to being distracted and led astray in order to avoid pain. If you are not connected to a healthy and Christ-honoring community, pray and ask God to lead you to one where you may continue to grow in the knowledge and grace of Christ. If you have been hurt by others both inside and outside of the church's walls, ask God for wisdom, discernment, and divine appointment for safe people to be God's hands and feet in your Dark Night. Continue reading the gospel of John and Isaiah chapters 40-66. Pray for someone who is struggling with life's challenges. Come alongside and encourage them with appreciation, affirmation of their gifts and talents and acknowledgment of their struggles in their journey.

---

64 www.cancersurvivors.org/Coping/end%20term/stages.htm.

CHAPTER 15

The Gift of Choice within Limitations (C)

My testimony—"After 30 years of being in different leadership positions and living in seven countries, God took me out of active pastoral ministry in 2004 and moved us 1,300 miles away. What I thought was a much needed but short sabbatical turned into a time of inactivity that seemed to drag on forever. There were ministry opportunities available, but God would not let me accept them. I was getting more and more frustrated, until one morning during one of our weekly grocery shopping trips to an Asian market. My heart was in turmoil as I was pushing the shopping cart behind Vivian. I finally cried out to God, "I don't care if you will ever use me in ministry again. I don't care if you will ever use the gifts, talents, and experiences you have given me. If you put me on the shelf for good, I am going to set my heart on walking with you for the rest of my life." The relief was almost instantaneous and the intimacy of God's presence and peace was quickly restored. But this same lesson had to be learned again and again."

As I look back over the past ten years of learning and growing in surrendering and accepting God's plan, I can see God was preparing our hearts for the needed inner strength to deal with several major family crises. Even in my struggles, doubts, and frustrations, God was fulfilling His purpose in my life. Through the move and the selling of our former home, God made provision for our family's physical needs. God also blessed us with long-term financial stability that overwhelms us with thankfulness. Vivian had the opportunity to finish her master's degree in Christian Studies. In the last six years we have had the blessed privilege of coming alongside pastors and missionaries in their DNX. Ten years after what we thought was a short sabbatical, this book was birthed from the wisdom, love, and grace of God to bless me, my family, and most of all, you, fellow sojourners of the DNX.

Limitations in life

All of us live with limitations in life. Some limitations are inherent from birth. Others are imposed on us by life circumstances, like DNX. After being blamed for a horrendous naval failure in WWI, Winston Churchill was fired from his post as Lord of the Admiralty. He was ostracized and ridiculed as an outcast and spent most of the next 20 years in a political wilderness. Later, in WWII, he became the Prime Minister of England. American president Franklin Delano Roosevelt contracted adult polio and could not walk or take care of his basic daily needs without personal help. Both of these political figures walked through their DNX making true grit choices within the limitations imposed on them. Having been molded by the choices they made in their painful experiences, they were instrumental in leading the Allies to victory in WWII. As I mentioned in chapter 13, King David committed grievous sins many times and yet he was called a man after God's own heart. Instead of running away from God as life unraveled, David chose to run toward God with contrition, honesty, and humility, fulfilling God's purpose for him in his generation.

Caution: Do not let one ugly event define you and the rest of your life. Do not let other people's opinion, betrayal, and abandonment dictate your future. We may not be able to change others and past wrongs but we can make changes in our own life, even within life's limitations and struggles. God has given us this gift of choice, because of, as well as in spite of, limitations.

The gift of choice (C) within limitations

In DNX we are confronted by many confusing and difficult choices. In reality there is one basic choice we can make that is always the best option. It is the choice of being the branch that abides in the vine through every season, especially during the dark and dreary season of winter. Choosing to abide means the branch is connected to the life source of the vine under the loving, tender care of the gardener, our heavenly Father (Jn 15:1). The branch is not responsible for the rainfall or sunshine or the growth of its leaves but only for abiding and staying connected to the vine. This act of abiding involves fellowshipping with God through prayer and being immersed in the Word of God (Jn 15:7). To abide is to invite God's presence to control and reign over all areas of life. This choice will lead to the fulfillment of the branch's deepest longing and its one and only purpose of existence, which is to bear fruit and lots of it (Jn 15:5, 16)!

Joni Eareckson Tada wrote, "With profound potential for good, suffering can also be a destroyer. Suffering can pull families together, uniting them through hardship, or it can rip them apart in selfishness and bitterness… It all depends. On us. On how we respond."[65]

DNX is likened to the winter of the heart when there is pruning and more pruning and waiting and more waiting. Do you know that the heavenly Father, the loving and skillful gardener, is closest to the branch, us, when He is pruning it? DNX is a time of deep losses when branches are trimmed back to the bare bones of the vine with nothing to show forth. It is both humbling and painful. The bare and snarly branches may look ugly for a season, but spring and fruitfulness are around the corner as it continues to abide in the vine. The same is true for our life. Count on it! John 15:5 says, "I am the vine; you are the branches. If a man remains in me and I in him, he *will* bear much fruit." (Italics added)

Examples of making choices within limitations

Betrayed and sold by his own brothers, Joseph became a slave and then a prisoner in a foreign country, alone and defenseless (Gn 37, 39-40). Under these limitations, Joseph chose to live as a branch with the vine, resolving to walk and abide in God's presence in faith and obedience. God later honored Joseph publicly and through him saved many lives (Gn 50:20).

Out of the 12 spies and the rest of the people of Israel, Joshua and Caleb were the only ones in their generation committed

---

65 Joni Eareckson Tada; quoted by Phil Callaway, *Making Life Rich without Any Money*, 71.

to trusting God to enter the Promised Land. Outnumbered, Joshua and Caleb were stuck in the desert for 40 years (Dt 1). They chose to walk with God in the desert alongside those who put them there. They even called these stiff-necked people "my brethren." God was with Joshua and Caleb and rewarded them for their choices in a terrible and unfair situation not of their choosing. Others, like Moses, Job, Hannah, and Mary, also made similar choices in their DNX. "Choose for yourselves this day whom you will serve" (Jo 24:15).

Best Advice—"What do I do when I don't know what to do?"

As we learn to make this vital choice of abiding in Christ, we still have to make many other practical decisions from day to day. A simple question of "what do you want for dinner" may easily stymie the best of us when we are in the thick of dealing with turmoil and pain. Others never move forward because they keep revisiting the decisions they made or failed to make before. The best advice from Elizabeth Elliot to help us move forward through our DNX is, "Do the next right thing."

I realize that in DNX some of us struggle just to get out of bed or leave the house without looking like someone living in the rough. During the early days of my DNX, I struggled to maintain the same pace I was previously keeping. I started making a "do list." When nothing got done, I made a "must-do list." Eventually, I was happy just to get out of bed and get one thing done a week. Learning to continually adjust expectations of ourselves is an important exercise and the right thing to do, especially during the early months of DNX. As I slowly regained strength and perspective, I could then tackle what I needed to do a little bit more each day and each week. In

DNX we need to create a new normal and a new rhythm for ourselves. Don't fight your tiredness. Sleep if you need to but do some walking or exercise each day.

When our energy is down and motivation nil, it is very tempting to feel useless. This is why it is so important to press in and stay connected to the vine, drawing our sustenance from being who we are in Christ, apart from what we do or fail to do. Don't complain, compare, or compete with your past performance. Stop beating yourself up or letting others beat you up emotionally. Humble yourself and solicit help and support from the safe people around you. There were times in my DNX when I could not even read the Bible. Either Vivian would read the Word out loud to me, or I would listen to audio Bible readings on my own. For many of you, Christian music may serve the same purpose in your DNX.

We need to be reminded not to compare and compete with others, even in the healing process during DNX. How and when healing takes place is unique with each individual, even though certain principles for healing hold true in all contexts. One survivor of 9/11 said, "In the seven years since the loss of my wife, there are times when a statement by someone, or a song, or a TV program still brings tears to my eyes."

So go at your own pace. Tackle one task, one decision, one day, one step at a time. Don't forget to daily celebrate victories no matter how small. "What's for dinner?"

Robert Louis Stevenson—"Don't judge each day by the

harvest you reap but by the seeds you plant."[66]

Amy Poehler — "Focus on what you have and do not be obsessed with what you don't have. You will be happier." (*ABC Nightline*, Oct. 19, 2012).

Robert Schuller — "Let a hopeful heart, not a hurting (or a hateful) heart drive you."

Jesus —"Therefore do not worry about tomorrow, for tomorrow will worry about itself. Each day has enough trouble of its own" (Mt 6:34).

Decision making in DNX

Avoid making any major decisions in the early days of a DNX until your heart is settled down in peace and quietness with God. I have seen many who made major life decisions at this unfavorable time and ended up worse off afterward with irreparable outcomes. However, when time does come for these major decisions, I am reminded of the words spoken by the founder of The Navigators Ministry, Dawson Trotman, "We do not have to see the whole staircase to take the first step." He also advised, "If you can't see very far ahead, go ahead as far as you can see." Slow and steady is essential in breaking through DNX as you apply God's truths to your life.

A summary testimony of John Bunyan

John Bunyan was born in 1628 in the little village of Elstow, in Bedfordshire, England, to a poor tinker father, "My descent

---

66   www.brainyquote.com/quotes/authors/r/robert_louis_stevenson.html

was of a low and inconsiderable generation, my father's house being of that rank that was the meanest and the most despised occupation of those days."[67] As a poor boy he could hardly read or write. "He was a ringleader of the village wickedness."[68] In his youth he enlisted as a soldier. He started to ponder about spiritual things and God but he could not change his ways. He almost drowned many times. At 19 he was married. His wife brought him two good books: *The Plain Man's Pathway to Heaven* and *The Practice of Piety*. He started to go to church but kept clinging to his sins and wickedness. Through preaching, his soul was wakened with conviction but not changed. One day in his cursing and carrying on, he was rebuked by the worst woman of the village. He once again determined to change his ways but there were no lasting results. The Spirit, through many means, kept drawing him to Christ with a growing conviction of sins.

One day, on the streets of Bedford as a tinker, he saw a few poor women sitting in a doorway conversing about the assurance of salvation, the preciousness of Christ as their personal savior, and the wretchedness of their human nature. He entered their conversation and sought counsel from them about his own state before God. They shared the gospel with him and he understood it for the first time. Bunyan started a series of conversations with these women to answer his many questions. Eventually, they had to refer him to their pastor, Mr. Gifford. His soul was deeply troubled through his studies of the scriptures. A book by Luther, *Treatise on Paul's Epistle to the Galatians,* came into

---

67   Alfred P. Gibbs (A Dreamer and his Wonderful Dream—the story of John Bunyan and 'the Pilgrim's progress.' Fort Dodge: Walterick Printing Company, 9-29. Cf. chapter 24 of Pilgrim's Progress, p.9.
68   Ibid., p. 10.

his possession. He valued this book next to his Bible, as he poured through the pages. One day, as he was passing through a field, a phrase was brought to his convicted consciousness, "Thy righteousness is in heaven." He saw for the first time the glorious truth of 2 Corinthians 5:21(KJV): "For God hath made Christ to be sin for us, He, Who knew no sin; that we might be made the righteousness of God in Him." All Bunyan's doubts were now dissolved like mist before the rising sun. He was baptized and joined a nonconformist, or dissenters, church, a church movement that was persecuted by the state church. He was later asked to preach on many occasions. He was jailed for 12 years in Bedford Prison, which was considered the most foul and loathsome place of confinement in England. He struggled with the condition of the prison, his indefinite imprisonment, and the lack of provision for his struggling family. He learned the deeper things of God in the solitude of prison life and wrote two of the books greatly used by God, *The Pilgrim's Progress* and *Grace Abounding to the Chief of Sinners*. For 16 years after his release he became a pastor who preached to thousands and influenced multitudes.

He died in 1688. The basic theme of his preaching was, "the all sufficiency of the living Word—Christ, and the 'written word'—the Scriptures, to meet all the needs of both sinner and saint."[69]

Actions (for personal and group study):

1. "As long as we want to be different from what God wants us to be at the time, we are only tormenting

---

69   Ibid., p. 27.

ourselves to no purpose."[70] Tell God honestly and humbly about your struggles with the limitations in your life.

2. Reflect on Psalm 32:8-9 again.

3. List three things you've learned so far from this book that encourages you.

---

70 Gerhart Tersteeegen, quoted in Ron Dunn, *When Heaven is Silent*, 23.

CHAPTER 16

The Gift of Re-creation (R)

Question—The dean of a seminary once asked me, "I thought I had successfully walked through my DNX, but how come shortly after I went back to work I was almost completely drained again?" At that instant God gave me an answer for him by showing him the following chart:

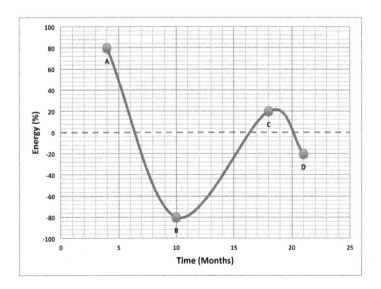

Explanation of the chart:

- **Point A** is our energy level before the onset of the Dark Night Experience (DNX).

- **Point B** is our energy level in the pit of the DNX.

- **Point C** is our energy level during the recovery process. At this point, many of us are eager to get back to work because our energy level has rebound 100% from a negative 80% to a positive 20%. When we do get back to work, we tend to be busy and forget the healthy lifestyle we have established in our recovery. Even though we may feel good and ready to go full throttle, our energy level is still at just 20% above zero. The stress and pressure of work will, in no time, drain our energy level back to zero or lower.

- **Point D** is where we may suddenly find ourselves tired and worn out soon after getting back to our regular work routine. Even with more sleep and getting back to regular exercise, we may still feel drained. It is God's way of reminding us again of the need for a more intentional and consistent change of lifestyle and the practice of wholesome self care of re-creation.

"Early to bed and early to rise, makes a person healthy, wealthy, and wise." Benjamin Franklin.

Testimony: Ron Dunn was run down, burned out, and depressed after the suicide of his son and his extended and demanding traveling ministry. Finally, he went to see the doctor about his prolonged bout with depression and his worsening health. The doctor started to tell him of his need for a change in lifestyle, including exercise and diet. Impatient to get well, Ron asked the doctor, "Can't you just give me a pill or something?" "The doctor picked up a notepad and began writing, 'I'm going to give you a list of things you need to start doing right now,' he said. 'First, I want you to walk three miles a day, four days a week. And do it in forty-five minutes. No dilly-dallying out there.' 'Second,' he said, 'I want you to eat at least two nutritious, well-balanced meals every day. Third, plan to get seven to eight hours of sleep every night. And remember, the hours before midnight are the best.'"[71]

The fifth gift is God's gracious gift of re-creation (R), the process of recreating and renewing us. God is in the process of recreating each of us daily as we walk through our DNX in His presence, moving us from despair to dignity. This process involves our body, soul, and spirit. I truly believe the application of this gift changed my life from inside out and outside in. I also know of people who never get over their Dark Night because of not applying grit to this gift. In the novel *Bourne Supremacy*, Bourne, the main character, was wrestling in his DNX with flashes of gruesome and fragmented images of his past. Dr. Mo, who diagnosed him as "a little more than a functioning vegetable," gave him the advice to "go do strenuous exercise" whenever he was pulled into that whirlpool of darkness.

We know that true healing or change comes from both inside out and outside in. The intense testing and trials in DNX deplete any physical, mental, or emotional reserve we may

---

71   Dunn, *Silent*, 25

have, to the point of emptiness. Like a gas tank that has sprung many leaks, we are driving around on empty with the warning light flashing. We wonder and worry if we have enough fuel to get to the next gas station without getting stuck somewhere. This gift of re-creation is God's amazing provision to plug up the leaks and refill our tank. I believe it is the fastest way to regain stability and equilibrium in DNX as we practice the GPS CROWN approach.

The apostle Paul testified to this make and break gift and grit in 1 Corinthians 9:26-27. "Therefore I do not run like a man running aimlessly; I do not fight like a man beating the air. No, I beat [i.e., *discipline*] my body and make it my slave so that after I have preached to others, I myself will not be disqualified for the prize." Paul knew that if he did not **discipline** his body he would eventually be disqualified from his calling. "Like a city whose walls are broken down is a man who lacks self-control" (Prv 25:28). A person who lacks self-control is vulnerable to temptations and deceptions that wreck and destroy life. The hard work of disciplining the body helps us develop self-control in other parts of our being.

Two other gifts complement the application of this gift of re-creation in order to confront the fears in our DNX—God's power and love. "For God did not give us a spirit of timidity, but a spirit of power, of love and of self-discipline" (2 Tm 1:7). While timidity, fear, and anxiety may paralyze us, acknowledging that we are loved and have access to the power of God empowers us to exercise self-discipline in DNX. Some years ago I was talking to a doctor-friend about a former paratrooper who was then in need of a knee and hip surgery. My friend's simple response was, "The body remembers." As I reflect again on his insightful answer, I realize the same principle applies to our inner world as well. Traumas leave their marks in our body, soul, and spirit even though we may have forgotten the specific incidents involved. To tap into God's gift of re-creation allows peace and wholeness to be restored. I am convinced that every day I spend aqua running is a good day.

A lighter note—After the first week of living at the university dormitory during summer school, I discovered my next-door neighbor, a football player, was always in the bathroom cubical with his notes and books. My curiosity was piqued and I finally asked him, "How come every time I am in the bathroom I always notice you in the cubical?" He smiled and said, "It is hard for me to concentrate and study. This is the only place I can concentrate." He had successfully found a way to become disciplined. Many graduate with honors but very few can claim they graduate with hemorrhoids. (Please chuckle!)

From personal experience—I never learned self-discipline in my childhood. The only way I survived the pain in my heart was to daydream, and that resulted in an undisciplined mind and life. In college, The Navigators taught me the practice of meditating and memorizing scripture. I discovered that the more I practiced these spiritual disciplines, the better I concentrated and had control over my thoughts. This control then extended to other areas of my life. "You will keep in perfect peace him whose mind is steadfast, because he trusts in you" (Is 26:3).

Vivian and I have been married for over 41 years. We went through thin and thick together. When we got married, I was

145 pounds. Then I began to gain weight at an average of 10 pounds a year. After over 40 years of marriage I should have been 545 pounds. About 18 years ago, at around 235 pounds, I developed diabetes, partly due to my love for sugary drinks and comfort food. The family sat me down and confronted me. Vivian was wise! She let our three daughters do all the talking. They asked, "Dad, do you want to serve God for a long time to come?" "Yes," I answered. "We want you to live a long life, too, dad," they continued. "You have to do something about your weight and deal seriously with your type II diabetes." The confrontation sobered me for a few days. Later on someone told me that I really did not have a weight problem but a height problem. "If you were ten feet tall you wouldn't have a weight problem." Who am I kidding?! It took 18 years of much learning, hard work, support, and encouragement to bring me to my present fighting weight. I may be fit for my age now but the damage to my body was already done. The doctor just warned me I might have to be on insulin soon if I don't live in the gym. Help!

Vivian goes to fitness class three times a week. I tried many types of exercise but eventually found great enjoyment in aqua running/walking/swimming. Over the years, Vivian had to learn to change her style of cooking and diet to accommodate my diabetes. It takes teamwork to keep fit and stay healthy; I certainly cannot do it on my own. Together we also commit ourselves to simplify all areas of our lives, living debt-free with less but enjoying life more.

Once my doctor-daughter asked me on the phone, "Dad, do you know you have a tendency toward depression?" I was momentarily stunned by her question. Up to then, I was not aware that I had that leaning. I always thought I was an easy-going guy. I then remembered how I came to know myself as an angry person when I was a young adult. Over time, this gift of re-creation, along with the other gifts and grits, continues to help me change from a driven, angry, and anxious person to one who is comfortable in his own skin. Through DNX I was forced to work through my past pain and be at ease with myself. The motto "pay now or pay later," with exorbitant interest like credit card debt, is true in life too. The longer we delay getting healthy and disciplined the heavier interest we will have to pay. No one gets away with it. Meanwhile, the diabetes, high blood pressure, and cholesterol have done their irreversible damage in my body.

How do you know if someone is depressed? According to Dr. Oz, if you walk into a room and spend a little time talking to a person, and when you leave the room you feel depressed, that person you were talking to is probably depressed. **What are the simple tests medical doctors use to determine if a person is depressed?** In the last two weeks have you had problems with your energy level, appetite, weight loss or weight gain, change in sleep pattern, concentration, feelings of apathy, or loss of love or zest for the hobbies in your life?

Principles/Suggestions to rebuild and maintain a healthy life style--

- If you do not have regular physical checkups, it is advisable that you have one done during DNX and inform your doctor of any physical, mental, or emotional issues with which you may be dealing. Don't be afraid to take medication until you regain your sense of equilibrium. It is quite alright if you need medication to sleep in your DNX. But also consider eating healthy foods and taking vitamin supplements. A diet rich in vegetables, fruit, multigrain, and white meat (chicken/turkey/fish) is good for overall health in any season of life.

- Don't hesitate to seek a second opinion and other alternatives in dealing with a health concern. I drink chamomile tea two hours before bedtime to help me sleep.

- Do exercise that you enjoy and that energizes you. It is best to do an activity that also occupies your mind to keep from thinking too much. During one of our DNX episodes Vivian learned quilting with a group of neighborhood ladies. During another DNX she took pottery lessons. These activities saved her sanity and mine too. Solitude can also be considered an activity if spent in a healthy and life affirming way. Reading a good book, taking long walks, listening to music, visiting a museum, learning a new hobby, etc. may all be done alone or with a good friend, especially in tough and dark seasons of life.

- Dr. Larry Crabb said in one of his class lectures, "Concerning stress, not everything is a ten-foot drop. Sometimes it is just a trip and a stumble to the ground." To help us adjust our emotional stress level, we may ask the question, "What is the worst case scenario in this situation?" Not all stress is harmful, as a matter of fact. Most of the time pain in stress helps us make necessary changes when nothing else can.

- To apply this gift of R and walk the GPS CROWN pathway daily, we need others to encourage and support us, like an exercise class, AA, family members, and close friends.

- Develop a hobby that fills you up physically, mentally, and emotionally. It will literally save your life. "You see, in life, lots of people know what to do, but few people actually do what they know. Knowing is not enough! You must take action."—Tony Robbins[72]

- Three R's from Dr. Oz: Rigorous daily activities; Real food—food from the ground; and Re-examine one's purpose in life, short and long term. From my perspective, occasional indulgence in something you enjoy may not be a bad thing. Sugar-free dark chocolate in strict moderation is the thing for me. What's yours?

Actions (for personal and group study):

1. "Do you not know that your body is a temple of the Holy Spirit, who is in you, whom you have received from God? You are not your own; you were bought at a price. Therefore honor God with your body." (1 Cor 6:19-20)

2. Start doing daily exercise.

3. Take small but definite steps to make your body the temple of the Holy Spirit, as God intends it to be.

4. Give thanks for what God has done for you in Christ.

---

72   http://sourcesofinsight.com/tony-robbins-quotes

CHAPTER 17

The Gift of One for All and All for One (O)

Reuben Welch said, "With God, even when nothing is happening—something is happening."[73]

Testimony—A missionary friend was walking through the early stages of her DNX, struggling with losses on several fronts. On her way back from church one Sunday, she saw a picture in her mind of what she was going through in her DNX. (Some may call this a vision.) In the scene, a truck is speeding down a steep hill and is forced to turn into the runaway lane to ease into a full stop. Being able to frame her recent and present DNX experiences with this mental picture, she gained a handle on understanding and engaging her struggles and inactivity. To shift gears is absolutely necessary for those of us who are addicted to busyness and activities. This is important for our own self-care and for finishing well in our calling.

There are two parts to this God-given gift of (O): **o**ne for all; all for **o**ne.

---

73   Dobson, *Sense*, 49.

Part I: One for all

The *one* refers to the one or more spiritual gifts given to each believer in Christ for the common good of **all**, the Body of Christ (1 Cor 12:4-7). There are four aspects to this spiritual gift:

1. "There are different kinds of gifts, but the same Spirit." (Different **gifts**)

2. "There are different kinds of service, but the same Lord." (Different **service**)

3. "There are different kinds of working, but the same God works all of them in all men." (Different **effect**)

4. "Now to each one the manifestation of the Spirit is given for the common good."(One **aim)**

God has given each of us different gifts, different places of service, and varying degrees of effectiveness, but with the same aim to facilitate growth and the building up of the Body of Christ (Eph 4:16).

At our first overseas assignment, I sensed that God wanted us to leave the ministry we were first assigned to because it was not consistent with my gifts, calling, and the burden I had for being on the mission field. The national director who oversaw the work threatened to send us home. As we sought God's counsel in prayer, we concluded, "God was the One who sent us to this country. We are staying with or without the financial support or the blessing of the national leader." When our missions director back home heard of the impasse, he wrote, "I am 100% behind John and Vivian doing what God is calling them to do. Go seek out another ministry within the field."

During this painful and chaotic transition, the uncertainties, stress, and anxieties triggered our first DNX. As we worked through the tormenting grief (Part I of this book), God opened amazing doors of ministry for me to preach, teach, and counsel. I preached at least twice at an Egyptian Coptic church. I also encountered incredible witnessing opportunities that bore amazing fruit. I was encouraged and energized by seeing God's hand still at work in and through me.

Meanwhile Vivian was taking her well-deserved time of rest and renewal at home. Eventually God sent us to plant a church 600 miles away. God brought about a small revival. In four years, the church plant grew from a handful of people to three congregations totaling 400 people. This was a very rare happening in that country, where the average attendance of the majority of well established evangelical churches hovers at around 100 people or less.

When we started the church plant, Vivian and I had a few arguments because I felt that she was holding back from engaging fully in the work. A few months later I was very close to being burned-out that I had to scale back my activities. Having been energized from her rest, Vivian was able to fill in the gap and put to full use the gifts she has from God. She carried me, the family, and the ministry, along with a deep sense of joy and fulfillment. I have learned since that God's healing process and timing is different and unique for each of us according to our personality and giftedness. His blessings will flow when we begin to understand and live out the attitude of poverty, purity, and privilege. (Chapter 14)

Part II—All for one

There is an overall confidence that undergirds our healing process in DNX; the second half of this gift of *O* is that confidence. "And we know that in **all** things God works for the good of those who love him, who have been called according to his purpose. For those God foreknew he also predestined to be conformed to the likeness of his Son, that he might be the firstborn among many brothers" (Rom 8:28-29).

These verses tell me that if I choose right here and now to love, obey, and trust God, He is able to make "all things"— the good, the bad and the ugly—work out for my ultimate good. This promise is for all who love God, regardless of what happened in our past. Our gracious and sovereign God is able to work, to fashion, and to weave together all things in our experiences for our good and His eternal purpose.

I once heard a woman speaker who used a piece of needle work to illustrate this truth. She first showed us the underside of a piece of cross-stitch made up of a jumbled mess of different colored threads. There was no way to know what was on the topside until she turned the cloth over. We never could have conjured up the beautiful pattern by simply looking at the bottom side. She then made two points.

1. We will never understand the pattern of God's way and work by only looking at it from our earthly perspective—the underside of the cross-stitch. "A man's steps are directed by

the LORD. How then can anyone understand his own way?" (Prv 20:24).

2. God is the consummate artist-at-work, who is more than able to incorporate any stains and mistakes into His overall design for our lives. A black dot may become the center of a sunflower. A yellowing stain may form the background of a sunset.

Let us learn more about this wonderful promise in Romans 8:28-29.

Romans 8:28-29 does NOT say:

- "Everything that happens to people is good." (They are not. Some are very bad.)

- "Whatever happens to us is good for us." (Depends on what "good" is and where we are spiritually with God.)

- "God will work out everything for everyone's good. (Only for those who love, obey, and trust Him.)

- "God is the cause of all the bad things that happen to us in the world." No, God is not. God is not the author of evil or temptation. Both our sin and Satan's interference are culpable. James 1:13-14 is clear: "When tempted, no one should say, 'God is tempting me.' For God cannot be tempted by evil, nor does he tempt anyone; but each one is tempted when, by his own evil desire, he is dragged away and enticed."

- "What is bad will eventually work out for my good." (However, we may not see it in our life time.)

What then does Romans 8:28-29 say?

1. "And we know"—the word *know* communicates conviction and certainty from personal experience. This is a living reality for Apostle Paul and many saints of past and present.

2. "In all things"— In the context of the verses before and after, *all things* refers to our sufferings, like troubles, pressures, hardship, persecution, famine, nakedness, sword, danger, etc. (Rom 8:35-39). When compared to the coming glory of God, these *all things* are, at best, "light and momentary... achieving for us an eternal glory that far outweighs them all" (2 Cor 4:17; cf. Rom 8:18).

3. "God" is the **One** who knows and understands our sufferings. In our DNX, Jesus is our "merciful and faithful high priest ... Because he himself suffered when he was tempted, he is able to help those who are being tempted" (Heb 2:17b-18) and "sympathize with our weaknesses" (Heb 4:15).

4. "Works together"—God guarantees that He will redeem and fashion everything in our lives for our good. Regardless of where we were and are in life's journey, nothing in our past or present experiences will be wasted or lost under God's powerful working hand. God is able to weave, to fit together, and to use every

part of what we know and learn for our good, for His glory, and for Kingdom work.

5. "For the good"—God's plan is never for evil but for our highest good, giving us a future and hope (Jer 29:11). Like Job in the Old Testament, sometimes our earthly and material loss may be restored to some measure in time. But the "good" that God is bringing out is primarily for our present and eternal hope of being made more like Christ with no regrets (Rom 8:29).

6. For whom is God working together all things? Only for "those who love him, who have been called according to his purpose" (Rom 8:28) to be "conformed to the likeness of His Son" (Rom 8:29). *Are you willing and ready to start loving and trusting Him?*

What a privilege it is to know that God, in His unconditional love, chose, called, and predestined us to know Him and receive the grace He lavishes on us (Eph 1:4b-8). Once in a while God may turn the cross stitch over and show us a glimpse of His sovereign design. In that brief moment of revelation, even though we do not see it clearly (1 Cor 13:12), we marvel at His wisdom, goodness, and mercy in our lives. "Oh, the depth of the riches of the wisdom and knowledge of God! How unsearchable his judgments, and his paths beyond tracing out!" (Rom 11:33).

Testimony of George Verwer:

"I remember a great failure in my own life through which God disciplined me. I was living in Spain, but I was studying

Russian because my great vision was for the Muslim and Communist worlds. In the summer of 1961 I headed for Moscow with a vehicle full of well-hidden Scriptures. You have heard of Brother Andrew, known as God's Smuggler. Well, I was God's Bungler! The summer ended with us being arrested by KGB and the Russian newspapers reporting, 'American Spies Caught.' After a couple of days of interrogation, they decided we were religious fanatics and gave us a submachine gun escort to the Austrian border. It was after that fiasco, in a day of prayer, that the bigger vision and idea came to me with the name Operation Mobilization. Once again by God's grace, in the midst of failure, something great was born that was to explode spiritually across the world. After failure, do you sometimes feel you have missed Plan A for your life? If you do, then thank God for His sovereignty and the reality of Romans 8:28: 'We know that in all things God works for the good of those who love him, who have been called according to his purpose.' Plan B or C can be just as great as Plan A. You may think that you have made a lot of mistakes and taken a lot of wrong turns in your life. Perhaps you feel you are on Plan F or G. I say, "Praise God for a big alphabet" and press on! No matter how much heartbreak, disappointments, and difficulties there may be, we need to keep a positive, grace-awakened attitude and keep moving forward in our response to the call of Jesus to be His witnesses throughout the world."[74]

Actions (for personal and group study):

1. Memorize, meditate, and pray Romans 8:28-29 into your life.

---

74   George Verwer. Out of the Comfort Zone, 34

2. Write and compare notes on what these verses teach and what they do not teach. Bring these truths to God in prayer.

3. Thank God that He is making all things to work out for your good as you make a firm decision to honor Him right here and right now and to make Jesus the Lord and savior of your life.

CHAPTER **18**

The Gift of a Wounded Healer[75] (W)

Testimony: In June 2011, the co-anchor of a Christian TV ministry shared her DNX in an interview. She recalled having an extra-marital affair while she and her husband were in full-time ministry. A child of mixed race was born as a result. She openly admitted how she was feeling at the time. "I absolutely cannot live through this. ... The pain was so great for me and for my husband. ... I don't live month by month but moment by moment. ... God's grace is able to restore any situation. ... God's promise of 'My grace is sufficient for you' (2 Cor 12:9) is absolutely true." God was using the co-anchor to comfort many who are facing similar DNX as wounded healers.

Who can really minister to the deeply wounded? Many of us foolishly think that our wounds disqualify us from our hopes, dreams, and usefulness. The opposite is true. God is able to make all things, even those that cause our DNX, work together for our good and His purpose. Our healing wounds

---

75 Carl Jung used the term 'wounded healer' to describe the phenomenon of a counselor and counselee relationship.

become the theme of our God-given life message to encourage others. Instead of being a wounded hater or victim, we can bless others by giving the gift of ourselves as a wounded healer.

Jesus "was despised and rejected by men, a man of sorrows, and familiar with suffering. Like one from whom men hide their faces he was despised, and we esteemed him not. Surely he took up our infirmities and carried our sorrows, yet we considered him stricken by God, smitten by him, and afflicted. But he was pierced for our transgressions, he was crushed for our iniquities; the punishment that brought us peace was upon him, and by his wounds we are healed" (Is 53:3-5).

Testimony of Helen Ling (Vivian's beloved mother)

Helen was born in 1917 in Amoy, China, as the eldest in a family of 2 girls and 6 boys. As far as we know her grandfather was the first ordained Christian minister in the area. Helen had the rare privilege of attending university, where she received a degree in music and a minor in English. At age 26 she married her sweetheart Kenneth, a fellow Christian in the church. According to custom, she moved into the Ling's family home in an era when family life was steeped in the old traditional ways. Besides having her own career as a music teacher, she had the added burden of running a demanding and large household where her patience and good will were tested daily. The 1940s were a time of war and unrest in China. During the long and lean years under Japanese occupation, Helen helped out with household finances through teaching private music lessons. Kenneth was not in good health while he was working for the American consulate.

In 1949 the communist forces were steadily moving south to take full occupation of China. The family had no choice but to evacuate. The last three ships were jammed with people leaving Amoy harbor when they were bombed. One escaped damage, one sank, and the one Kenneth and Helen were on was crippled. Instead of heading to Taiwan by crossing the channel as planned, the crippled vessel had to make a quick getaway, hugging the coastline until they reached Hong Kong. Soon after they landed as refugees, Kenneth's health deteriorated quickly. At the hospital, the doctor was preparing Helen for the imminent passing of her husband of 6 years. Helen pleaded with God for healing but God did not answer that prayer. At the end of three weeks, Helen was finally ready to accept God's will and release her beloved husband to God. Only then did God take Kenneth to his heavenly home. With a heavy heart and the daunting task of raising two girls, a 2-year-old and a 7-month-old with only $5 left to her name, Helen knelt and entrusted herself to her living and loving Savior in a city that spoke an entirely different dialect than the one she knew. Her pain of loss was made even worse when she was blamed for her husband's death, as he was everyone's favorite and the first of his generation to die.

According to custom, Helen spelled bad luck for the family. Yet through all those early years of misunderstanding and prejudice, Helen refused to be bitter and resentful. Instead she turned to God, who saved her during high school years under the ministry of Dr. John Sung. Her faith in God sustained her as she raised her children in post-war Hong Kong. She continued to extend good will to family members and eventually won them over years later. Some have put their personal faith in Christ because of her.

God opened a door for her to teach music at a Christian high school. She volunteered to teach voice and piano at The Alliance Bible College on Cheung Chau Island and helped develop the music ministry for Far East Broadcasting Company in Hong Kong and Asia. She was called "Mommy Chen" by many of her students at the Bible College. She was especially dear to students from other parts of Southeast Asia who were far from home and in need of encouragement and motherly care.

Her unselfish generosity continued to be remembered long after graduation. Many students came to San Francisco from other parts of the world just to thank and bless her with visits and gifts. Her voice, which carried messages of hope and freedom, was heard all over China through Christian broadcasting during the closed-door years. As a teacher both in high school and Bible school, she not only taught music but also lessons in faith, love, and hope, blazing a trail and leaving behind a legacy in the lives of all who knew her.

In every church John and Vivian served, Helen made a special effort to befriend the widows; these friendships lasted throughout the rest of her life. As a mother to her daughters, she was selfless in giving her all, even her personal happiness, to raise them in a safe and comfortable environment. She was comforted in knowing that God had answered her prayer for the salvation of her children. She was also tireless in giving of herself to bless and intercede for her grandchildren and great grandchildren.

Helen rested from her earthly labor on February 6, 2013, at the age of 96. Her life had been a testimony of God's sovereign goodness and power. Through all the pain and suffering from tragic losses, danger, poverty, slander, loneliness, and ill health, God equipped her to be a wounded healer who influenced lives for God around the globe.

(John: Toward the very end of her life, one of the most unforgettable scenes for me was seeing our doctor-daughter kneeling by Helen's bed and taking care of her much-loved grandma with unbelievable gentleness, love, and tears.)

Three memorial services were held in Hong Kong and North America to celebrate her life and the legacy she left behind. She was truly the wounded healer who was **"sorrowful, yet always rejoicing; poor, yet making many rich; having nothing, and yet possessing everything"** (2 Cor 6:10).

As a result of a diving accident at the age of 15, **Joni Eareckson Tada** has been living ever since as a paraplegic. In her late 40s, she had this to say about despair and heart-wrenching questions. "Despair that rises in a direct and vertical line to God opens us up to change, real hope, and the possibility of seeing God as he really is, not as we want him to be."[76] And "heart-wrenching questions expose false hopes. And hopes that are false should be blown to smithereens."[77]

Choosing to move on with life does not mean excusing the wrong doer or ignoring the wrong committed. Do not misinterpret Jesus's teaching of loving your enemy as a license to be a doormat or punching bag for others to abuse and mistreat. Also, be aware of nursing a victim mentality that causes us to

---

76   Joni Eareckson Tada, *When God Weeps* (Grand Rapids: Zondervan 1997), 157.
77   Ibid., 154.

be self-centered, self-absorbed, entitled, and miserable. We don't have to be driven by the attitude that says, "I am mistreated and hurt. It is not fair. I do not deserve it. I have this great big hole in my heart. You should cater to me because I am in pain. I have the right to be bitter and act the way I do. I am entitled to get my way."

Wounded healer is an oxymoronic phrase that makes me sit up and take notice. It speaks of pain and hurt, healing, and purpose in one breath. The apostle Paul used the term *comforter* to describe a wounded healer: "Praise be to the God and Father of our Lord Jesus Christ, the Father of compassion and the God of all comfort, who comforts us in all our troubles, so that we can comfort those in any trouble with the comfort we ourselves have received from God. For just as the sufferings of Christ flow over into our lives, so also through Christ our comfort overflows" (2 Cor 1:3-5).

The word *comfort* consists of two meanings: coming alongside and adding strength. By lending strength, comfort, and encouragement, a wounded healer is a fellow wounded sojourner that comes alongside to help another to keep on keeping on.

I struggled for many years to understand what encouragement is? I have finally come to see encouragement in three strands: acceptance, appreciation, and affirmation. How can I be an encourager to others? I encourage others when I communicate by word or deed my heart-felt acceptance and appreciation of who and where they are in life. I affirm others by active listening and highlighting to them what God may be doing in their lives. There is a saying by Joyce Meyer, "Hurting people *hurt* people."[78] A wounded victim ends up being a wounded hater, causing pain in others. However, a wounded healer is someone who is a hurting but *healing* person.

How did Paul become a wounded healer? (Read 2 Cor 12:1-10)

1. The wound—Some suffer from self-inflicted wounds, others from other-inflicted wounds, or just life-inflicted wounds. It is most hurtful when we suffer from wounds inflicted by fellow Christians or spiritual leaders. Paul's wound came from a blessed experience ordained by God 14 years before when he was caught up to the third heaven, to paradise, where he "heard inexpressible things, things that man is not permitted to tell" (12:2, 4). To protect Paul from being conceited God allowed a "thorn in the flesh" to inflict Paul. A "thorn" is a wooden stake like those used to stake the ropes for a tent. To be inflicted by a thorn was likened to being impaled by a wooden stake. Some biblical scholars believe Paul's suffering was due to some eye disease.

2. Satan seized the moment of Paul's affliction and tormented and pummeled him (12:7).

3. Paul lived with this excruciating pain for 14 years, until the end of his life.

4. What did Paul do about the pain? He prayed three times for healing and three times God's answer to him was "no" (12:8). Does it mean God does not care or is powerless to intervene? Of course not, because

---

78   http://joycemeyer.org/Articles/EAARCHIVE.aspx?tag=relationships

God did answer Paul's prayer, though not his specific request. God gave Paul something far more eternally valuable than temporary healing. God gave Paul a promise of His rest—His presence and His peace, and the honor of becoming a wounded healer or a comforter to millions upon millions through his letters.

5. In the throes of the excruciating pain of living with an "impaled stake," Paul was assured of God's promise, "My grace is sufficient for you, for my power is made perfect in weakness" (12: 9). Paul came to see that all the insults, hardships, persecution, and difficulties he endured were opportunities to boast of his weaknesses and show off God's power (12: 9-10). In our DNX our weaknesses, insufficiencies, shame, and pain are often magnified. Paul is reminding us that this is our opportunity to boast and not curse or complain about our weaknesses, so that God's presence, power, grace, and peace can be manifested in and through us—the beginning of true freedom in Christ.

6. Augustine's mother prayed that her son would not go to Rome to live a decadent lifestyle. God did not answer her prayer then. Only later did God answer her prayer in bringing Augustine to salvation in Rome. *God answers prayer without answering prayer.* Saying "no" to Paul's prayer for healing was God's way of answering Paul's deeper longing of the heart. Acknowledging God's sovereign wisdom, Paul bowed his will to accept God's answer of "no" and acted on God's promise of "yes" by boasting of his pain and weaknesses.

7. Like Paul, "rejected by men, accepted by God" summarized G. Campbell Morgan's life and ministry. Earlier he was rejected by a denomination to preach and pastor but later became the prince of preachers and was greatly used by God. This is the training and experience of a wounded healer to become a comforter to others.

Actions (for personal and group study):

1. What has this chapter added to your understanding of the DNX?

2. If God is saying "no" to your specific prayer, be humble and ask God to open your eyes and ears to His "yes" as you review Psalm 32:8-9 and 2 Corinthians 12:9-10. Bring these verses to God in prayer.

CHAPTER 19

The Gift of NCR (N)

A shocking surprise in DNX-- during DNX it is common for God to withhold the manifestation of His gifts to us for a period of time. In other words, God is hiding His hand, the victorious "hand of God" that does His work through our spiritual gifts. His purpose is threefold:

- To drive us to seek the face of God in a deeper way. "Your face, Lord, I will seek" (Ps 27:8).

- To test our hearts to worship only God, the giver, and not the gifts. "Dear children, keep yourselves from idols" (1 Jn 5:21).

- To put steel into our backbone by learning to stand up against unjust criticisms and ignorant accusations when many have been criticized for not having enough faith to get out of their Dark Night. Others are accused of loss of faith, or loss of anointing as the cause of their DNX. When God withholds the use of our spiritual gifts for a season, it is always for our long term blessing and fruitfulness as He prepares us for the next phase of our life and ministry.

This last gift of NCR is the gift of boundary for our protection and sanity. "A boundary is a personal property line that marks those things for which we are responsible. In other words, boundaries define who we are and who we are not. They impact all areas of our lives…Having clear boundaries is essential to a healthy, balanced lifestyle."[79] Someone has said, "Good boundaries make good neighbors." The opposite is also true that bad boundaries make bad neighbors and relationships. Especially as we journey through our Dark Night, this wonderful gift of NCR will give us the confidence that God's grace is more than sufficient for the responsibilities He assigns to us. It also sets us free from entanglements, unrealistic expectations, unreasonable cultural demands, past pains, future fear, and the opinions of others.

The first letter N stands for none of my business. Do you know that there are secret things that only belong to God and things we can only know when they are revealed to us (Dt 29:29)? Do you know that there are many things we do not need to have an opinion on or to stick our beaks into? Do you know that God only requires us to take care of those things that we have been given the responsibility for and nothing else? If we think we have wisdom and insight in a matter, we do need to share it. Only in humility and with much prayer are we to share with those directly responsible and no one else. We certainly do not want to get entangled

---

79   Henry Cloud and John Townsend's book *Boundaries: When to Say YES, When to Say NO to Take Control of Your Life* (Grand Rapids: Zondervan 1992). Description given on dust jacket.

in complaining, criticizing, or gossiping behind people's backs.

After Peter's three denials and Jesus' resurrection, they met again by the Sea of Galilee over breakfast. Confronted by Jesus' penetrating questions and vision of his future, Peter seemed distracted or even evasive. "Peter turned and saw that the disciple whom Jesus loved was following them. ... [H]e asked, 'Lord, what about him?' Jesus answered, 'If I want him to remain alive until I return, what is that to you? You must follow me'" (Jn 21:20-22). In other words, Jesus was saying to Peter, "It is none of your business. You just follow me."

The way God leads each of us in life is as unique as our fingerprints. It is so sad to see people whose lives are in ruins because of their bad choices and poor judgments and yet have a proclivity to tell others how to live their lives. I do a lot of writing in cafes. I often unwittingly hear conversations around me. I would categorically say that the overwhelming majority of conversations, maybe even 90%, are filled with complaints, criticisms, and put-downs about someone or something. It is always revealing to hear the "wisdom" of the unemployables and the talk of "Monday morning quarterbacks." They rant and rave about the mistakes of others and how they could have done the same so much better. On a recent political election day I heard a granny loudly proclaim, "All politicians are liars and idiots. This is what he or she said and did ..." Then her grandson asked, "Who are you going to vote for, then?" She answered, "I am not going to vote for anyone. They are all crooks." As followers of Christ we are called to "[d]o everything without complaining or arguing, so that [we] may become blameless and pure, children of God without fault in a crooked and depraved generation" (Phil 2:14-15). How much energy are we spending on complaining about those "none of our business" items? They never fail to drain and distract us from fulfilling our God-given responsibilities.

The second letter C stands for concern. There are many things we are concerned about but have no control over, like the choices our adult children make, our parents' health habits, the work place decisions of our superiors, the conditions of the church and economy, etc. We know that if we say what we think, we may cause strain in or even breakup a relationship. We seriously need wisdom and grace to know what to do under these tenuous circumstances. Over the years, I have discovered four things we can do about our concerns. They are: prayer, trust, support, and distancing ourselves and/or direct intervention.'

Prayer and trust: We can pray by faith and trust that the Almighty God would intervene in the lives of those we are concerned about. People with problems tend to dump their problems on those of us who show we care. As "wounded healers" we need to be wise and not take on others' responsibilities in order not to hinder but help them mature in the long run. What we consider to be a loving gesture may well be keeping others from doing what is right. We are mistaken if we think it cruel and unloving to help others to be responsible. It is actually the best and most loving thing we can do for them because we are helping them to grow up and be successful in life. This is certainly true if you are a friend to someone in DNX. If you yourself are in the midst of DNX, know that God's provision is sufficient to handle your concerns and enable you to stay faithful to Him.

Support: In addition to our prayer and trust in God, the third thing we can do is to support and build trust with the one about whom we are concerned. Sooner or later all of us will need help, support, and counsel to deal with the challenges of life. In order to be well received, support and counsel need to be given at the right time and the right place. A friend once gave me this wise advice, "Never drive a ten-ton truck of truth over a five-ton bridge." Building trust in a relationship is a way of strengthening the bridge of communication in preparation for the ten-ton truth to be carried across the troubled water. This requires intentional investment of time and effort. Or else both the bridge and the truck of truth will collapse and be lost in the torrent.

Distance and/or direct intervention: One of the steps we can take about our concern may be to distant ourselves from the situation for a season because it has become toxic and hurtful to us. Or we may seek direct group intervention with much prayer and discernment. However, this last step may not be possible with people who refuse to take responsibility for their bad choices and actions and continue to use accusation and blame to justify their abusive and addictive behaviors. In such cases, the only recourse is to live with the stalemate by God's grace until there is a change of heart. It is a course of inaction that tests our patience and commitment to love, an exercise that is not pleasant but very maturing in Christ.

The third letter to describe boundaries is *R* for responsibility.

Like a property line, boundaries mark our responsibility with limits of what is included and excluded within those boundaries. "Your freedom ends where my nose begins," someone said. We need to be clear on where our personal responsibilities lie and stay within those limits without trespassing or meddling in someone else's affairs. To set boundaries regarding our own responsibility is to learn to say "yes," "no," "maybe," "later," and "help." It requires us to respect our own and others' boundaries so that we can experience order, freedom, and healthy relationships.

Conflict is bound to occur when one side refuses to accept set boundaries. One important area where we need boundaries is in our attempt to change others or to expect others to change. I have seen many frustrated and miserable people who spend much of their time trying to change others or expecting others to change. They end up living insane lives. Einstein is thought to have said, "Insanity is doing the same thing over and over and expecting a different result." [80] If a person has been consistently doing and acting a certain way for the past 20 years, don't expect change in the person overnight. The sooner we accept the fact that we can only change ourselves, the better we are able to enjoy life and have healthy relationships. Life is too short!

One important reality about responsibility is that it always requires resources and experiences that are beyond what we have. This is certainly true in DNX. To be responsible before God means to take up our God-given responsibilities and respond with our God-given ability and resources. It pleases God that we live by faith and obedience in total dependence on Him. "Faith is not necessarily the power to make things

---

80   However, "current consensus is that it came from the author Rita Mae Brown in her book Sudden Death on Pg. 68 from 1983." http://wiki.answers.com/Q/ Who first said that the definition of insanity is to do the same thing over and over and expect different results. Viewed Aug. 05, 2014.

the way we want them to be; it is the courage to face things as they are."[81] Living by faith and obedience often means facing impossible and risky situations with uncertain outcomes. From the lives of Shadrach, Meshach, and Abednego in the fiery furnace (Dn 3:1-30), we can learn four lessons (AARP) about walking by faith:

1. Able—Daniel's three friends know that God is *able* to deliver them. "O Nebuchadnezzar, we do not need to defend ourselves before you in this matter. If we are thrown into the blazing furnace, the God we serve is able to save us from it, and he will rescue us from your hand, O king" (3:16-17).

2. Ambiguity— "But even if he does not, we want you to know ..." (3:18). Not knowing for sure if God would save them from the furnace is not because of their lack of faith in God's goodness and power. It is part of a life of faith and obedience. Choosing to trust and obey God with ambiguity and uncertainty as to the outcome is a faith that pleases God.

3. Resolution—No matter what happens next, the three friends of Daniel already resolve not to bend their knees to idols. "[W]e want you to know, O king, that we will not serve your gods or worship the image of gold you have set up" (3:18).

4. Press forward—At the king's decree (3:4-7), Shadrach, Meshach, and Abednego already press forward in faith and resolve to obey God rather than worship the

---

81   Dunn, *Silent*, 46.

king regardless of the threat of being "thrown into a blazing furnace" (3:6). The king's decree and threat is out of their control and therefore none of their business (N). However, their lives and safety are certainly an immediate concern (C) though not theirs to dictate. The only decision or action they are responsible for (R) is their resolve to serve and worship God alone by faith. Someone explains "faith" using the acronym, "forward action inspired through Him," which acknowledges the fact that, "everyone who wants to live a godly life in Christ Jesus will be persecuted" (2 Tm 3:12).

Actions (for personal and group study):

1. Is there anything in the "none of your business" category that you need to stop doing'? Ask God for the grace to stop and change as you redefine your responsibilities.

2. What are any concerns for which you need to trust God and seek support?

3. What are the relationships that you need to distance yourselves from or confront?

4. What area(s) of your life requires you to live by faith, following the example (AARP) of Daniel's three friends (Dn 3:16-18)?

5. List three things you learned about God, His way, and yourself from the last few chapters.

CHAPTER 20

God's Leading after the Dark Night Experience

According to Martin Luther of the Reformation, when "God works in a way which is obviously consistent with His nature," it is referred to as "**the proper work of God.**" But when "God works in a way which **initially seems to contradict his nature**, yet on further reflection is seen to be totally consistent with it[,]" it is referred to as "the strange work of God [as in DNX]." [82] (Emphasis added). Through the winter of the heart God breaks down the strongholds in our hearts, heals our wounds, enables us to release our dreams to Him, instructs us to develop new disciplines, and helps us acquire wisdom while we walk in step with Him into the next phase of our lives. We are now in a place of contentment and acceptance without demanding our wants and wills. We are no longer rushing around to get out of the DNX but growing in perseverance and wholeness.

"**How do we know we have survived, revived, and thrived in our DNX?**" (2 Cor 1:3-11)

---

82   McGrath, *Suffering and God*, 34-35.

I see five signs in 2 Corinthians 1:3-11 that indicate someone has survived, revived, and thrived in his or her DNX: comfort, contentment, confidence, need for a community of prayer, and the ability to comfort others.

1. The word *comfort* means *coming alongside to add strength.* We know that we are moving into a new season of life when we have consistently experienced God's nearness and received His strength for dealing with guilt, grief, anger, anxiety, snares, stress, and shame (GAS). God, in his timing and ways, has identified the grieving issues in our soul and comforted us through His Word, promises, and assurance, as well as given us a future and a hope. Darkness always chases after deeper darkness, but only light, God's comfort, can dissipate darkness.

2. We know we have moved on from our DNX when we experience His **contentment,** but not complacency. We have come to see more clearly who God is and who we are in Christ. We have learned to entrust our desires and longing to God's will, purpose, and timetable. We are calmly waiting for God to open doors and close doors for the next step of our lives.

3. We have developed a **confidence** in Him that He is in complete control of every detail of our lives and is able to sustain us through troubles and sufferings. His unmerited and unlimited grace is more than sufficient to help us be more than conquerors in any and all circumstances.

4. We are growing in acknowledging our need for the help and support of a praying **community in our time of need.** We have learned to be vulnerable and transparent with safe people in our struggles in DNX. We no longer need to hide behind our pride and self-sufficiency.

5. We are able to **comfort others** in their DNX with the comfort God has comforted us (2 Cor 1:3-4).

The following is a very insightful paragraph written by Dr. Shelly Trebesch on God's leading after DNX or isolation. "One … must wait until God leads him/her out of the wilderness, for the temptation to leave before will always be present. When he was in the wilderness, Jesus ate nothing in his forty days of fasting and at the end of the time he was hungry. So the devil tempted him to make stones turn into bread—tempted him to eat. In isolation one is tempted to get satisfied, to get out of pain, out of isolation. Yet a premature departure from the desert may circumvent the refining/transforming process.

"As the reader will find in every biblical example of a person in isolation, and as we have found in most every case study we have explored, God eventually brings leaders out of isolation. He is faithful. There comes an intuitive point in which leaders begin to look toward the future. God, by his Spirit, gently gives persons permission to begin looking outward again for a return to ministry and to begin exiting the isolation period. Sometimes the Lord radically pulls leaders out of isolation, for example, by instigating their release from prison, bringing them through a paradigm shift, or by healing their sickness. More often, however, God quietly releases leaders to begin the process of exploring the next stage of their lives by sending a divine contact or an opportunity that matches their vision and the transformation that has occurred during the isolation period. Either way, the leader entering this phase will have a quiet peace when looking forward to the future, rather than a restless desire to escape the pain of isolation."[83]

How did God lead Naaman out of his DNX?—2 Kings 5:1-19

Naaman was a highly respected army commander, "a valiant soldier, but he had leprosy" (5:1). Naaman could not remove this scourge until an unlikely encounter in his own home.

1. God using unlikely people and situations to guide us (5:2-3)

In ancient times, a young girl taken into captivity as a slave in a foreign land had no rights or respect. Yet this particular young girl from Israel proved to be the unlikely life-changer or wounded healer in the life of the mighty warrior. She dared to voice her wish to her mistress, "If only my master would see the prophet who is in Samaria! He would cure him of his leprosy" (5: 3). She must have earned the trust of her mistress so that what she said was repeated to the master and through her master to the king himself. It was the beginning of a chain of events that eventually changed the landscape of Naaman's life.

2. Confronting our preconceived expectations and ideas of God's way (5:9-12)

Endorsed and encouraged by the king, Naaman proceeded to seek an audience with the prophet. "So Naaman went with his

---

83   Trebesch, *Isolation*, 42-43.

horses and chariots and stopped at the door of Elisha's house. Elisha sent a messenger to say to him, 'Go, wash yourself seven times in the Jordan, and your flesh will be restored and you will be cleansed'" (5:9-10). What? Is that all? Not only was Naaman humiliated and angry because the prophet of God did not even bother to show up to meet him, but also because the so-called cure was not at all what he expected. "I thought that he would surely come out to me and stand and call on the name of the LORD his God, wave his hand over the spot, and cure me of my leprosy. Are not Abana and Pharpar, the rivers of Damascus, better than any of the waters of Israel? Couldn't I wash in them and be cleansed? Humiliated and angry, Naaman turned around and went home in a rage" (5:11-12).

Here are some of my preconceived expectations about God's ways that had to be challenged:

1. I demanded that God should lead me back to where my life was before the DNX.

2. I expected God to lead me the way He led me in the past.

3. I anxiously looked about me (dismayed) for ways God should answer my prayer. His promise to me was, "So do not fear, for I am with you; do not be dismayed, for I am your God. I will strengthen you and help you; I will uphold you with my righteous right hand" (Is 41:10).

4. I was frustrated that God did not tell me what He was doing or not doing.

5. I was troubled with tomorrow's worries and not being thankful for what He had done already.

6. I demanded that God should use my talents, gifts, and experiences the way I wanted Him to. I thought waiting was a waste of time. My gifts, experiences, relationships, and skills ended up becoming a god that I worshipped.

7. I thought that it was not right for God to put me on the shelf for any length of time.

8. I lost sight of living by faith as a little child and being a servant that does his master's will.

9. I wanted God to open doors of ministry for me without taking the time to be changed and molded by Him. Impatience is immaturity.

10. I expected God to do things for me instead of learning to please Him by growing in discipline, diligence, and discernment.

3. Willingness to submit to God's direction even though it is counter intuitive (5:13-14)

It was a good thing that Naaman at least listened to reason. His servants approached him and said, "My father, if the prophet had told you to do some great thing, would you not have done it? How much more, then, when he tells you, 'Wash and be cleansed!' " (5:13). With nothing to lose, Naaman did as the man of God instructed. "So he went down and dipped himself in the Jordan seven times, ... and his flesh was restored and became clean like that of a young boy" (5:14).

4. Acknowledging God's work and living in the light (5:15-19)

"Then Naaman and all his attendants went back to the man of God. He stood before him and said, 'Now I know that there is no God in all the world except in Israel'" (5:15). Naaman further pledged his allegiance to God when he promised, "never again make burnt offerings and sacrifices to any other god but the LORD" (5:17b). Naaman also sought from the prophet forgiveness and understanding for his service to the king, "But may the LORD forgive your servant for this one thing: When my master enters the temple of Rimmon to bow down and he is leaning on my arm and I bow there also—when I bow down in the temple of Rimmon, may the LORD forgive your servant for this" (5:18).

Closing remarks—Ten years ago I was allergic to three things: writing, my cooking, and washing dishes. Writing this book has been one of the hardest things I have ever done. I wanted to quit many times, but God would not let me. Writing has developed in me discipline, diligence, and discernment that literally changed my life, my preaching, and my walk with God. As I reflect on the ending of this book on my upcoming 69th birthday, God is reminding me of two scripture passages that He gave me in the past.

The first one came 45 years ago during my sophomore year at university. I was part of a planning committee that organized a Christian retreat for international students. I arrived at the campground late Friday night for our first on-site meeting.

Early the next morning I walked out of the cabin into a thick fog as I searched for a place for my morning devotions. As I walked along a path I came to a turnoff lined with wooden planks. Following the planks I reached a drop-off point. I plunked myself down with my legs dangling over an unseen void. I then turned to my morning reading in John 7:37-38: "On the last and greatest day of the Feast, Jesus stood and said in a loud voice, 'If anyone is thirsty, let him come to me and drink. Whoever believes in me, as the Scripture has said, streams of living water will flow from within him.'"

A breeze was starting to part the fog. I saw that I was sitting on a pier over a gentle flowing river about a kilometer wide. An unfolding scene of clustered trees and various kinds of vegetation lay before my eyes and the breeze set my imagination aflame as I reflected on the scriptures I had just read. I imagined people stumbling down the banks and drinking thirstily from the river of living water—the weak, the poor, the lonely, the thirsty, the broken-hearted, and the addicted. Some were carried down by others. This river of living water was free for anyone and everyone. As promised, all who believe and put their total trust in Jesus will have their deepest thirst quenched and satisfied. "Whoever believes in me, as the Scripture has said, streams of living water will flow from within him. By this he meant the Spirit, whom those who believed in him were later to receive" (Jn 7:38-39). Moreover, out of our quenched hearts, rivers of living waters will flow through us to bring life and refreshment to the desolate, desperate, and despairing. On that early Saturday morning 45 years ago, the Holy Spirit created such a thirst in me that I committed my life once again to be controlled and filled by the Spirit for the fulfillment of this vision.

The second scripture came when God impressed upon my heart that if I continue to honor Him, He will fulfill in my life the verse that says, "No eye has seen, no ear has heard, no mind has conceived what God has prepared for those who love him" (1 Cor 2:9). Since our first Dark Night Experience 25 years ago, there were many more agonizing periods of Dark Nights. In every such experience God gave us the grace to run toward Him and not away from Him. We had many opportunities to walk on the gritty and lonely path of trusting and obeying like Abraham in Genesis 12, when he was "going and not knowing." My bondages began to lose their grip as I continued to grow deeper into God's Word by His Spirit. God has never failed or forsaken me over all these years. The refreshing living waters continue to nourish and energize my life for His purpose.

Vivian and I are so thankful for all those dark and wintery pruning seasons that are still bearing precious and juicy fruits in our golden years. Life for Vivian and I right now is both enjoyable and rich with meaning and purpose. We are humbled by His amazing and loving plans for us, which are way beyond our expectation. I pray that God will give us 15 more years to serve His Body, especially those seeking to plant His Church in the most challenging, dangerous, and desolate places of the world.

Now I am only allergic to two things: my cooking and washing dishes, but writing is still very hard work.

John Moy - M.Sc.Counseling; M.Div.; D. Min.(Candidate)
Vivian Moy - M.A. in Biblical Studies
CEO Pathfinder Partners
dnxpapa@gmail.com
www.icmsgo.com

Acknowledgments

To Bill and Alyce, Dave and Corrine, we thank you for giving us a solid start in our walk as followers of Jesus. The Lordship of Christ and the authority of God's Word remain the guiding forces that shape our lives and choices to this day.

To Jack and Carol, Gary and Dottie, we thank you for demonstrating the sufficiency of God's grace and power in the high calling of being the under-shepherd of God's flock.

To the past and present pastoral shepherds of NLCC church community, we thank you for welcoming us with opened arms and generous gifts of grace.

To our life group and our Sunday morning coffee group with the motto, "what happens in Timmy stays in Timmy," we thank you for sustaining and enriching us in prayer and in fellowship, through good times and dark nights.

To all the donors and prayer supporters, we thank you for

your partnership to make this book possible for the glory of our LORD.

Above all else, we owe our gratitude and all that we are, have, and do to Jesus the Christ, who saved and redeemed us for Himself and His purpose, the author and finisher of our faith. Through all our Dark Nights, He has shown Himself to be utterly good, steadfastly loving, unwavering faithful, and genuinely sovereign. May He be pleased and glorified by our offering of this book.

Bibliography

Andersen, Neil. *Victory over Darkness,* 2nd ed. Ventura: Regal Books, 2000.

Backus, William D. *The Hidden Rift with God.* Minneapolis: Bethany House Publishers, 1990.

Billheimer, Paul E. *Don't Waste Your Sorrows.* Fort Washington: Christian Literature Crusade, 1977.

Buchanan, Mark. *Spiritual Rhythm: Being with Jesus Every Season of Your Soul.* Grand Rapids: Zondervan, 2010.

Buchanan, Mark. *Your God is Too Safe: Rediscovering the Wonder of a God You Can't Control.* Colorado Springs: Multnomah Publishers 2001.

Chambers, Oswald. *My Utmost for His Highest: Selections for the Year.* New York: Dodd, Mead & Company, 1952.

Cloud, Henry and John Townsend. *Boundaries: When to Say YES, When to Say NO to Take Control of Your Life*. Grand Rapids: Zondervan Publishing Company, 1992.

Cloud, Henry and John Townsend. *Safe People: How to Find Relationships That Are Good for You and Avoid Those That Aren't*. Grand Rapids: Zondervan, 1995.

Colson, Charles, with Anne Morse, "My Soul's Dark Night." *Christianity Today*. December 2005, Vol. 49, No. 12, 80. www.christianitytoday.com/ct/2005/december/15.80.html.

Colson, Charles with Ellen Santilli Vaughn. *The Body: Being Light in the Darkness*. Dallas: Word Publishing, 1992.

Dobson, James. *When God Doesn't Make Sense*. Wheaton: Tyndale House Publishers, 1993.

Dunn, Ron. *When Heaven is Silent: How God Ministers to Us Through the Challenges of Life*. Milton Keynes: Authentic Publishing, 1994.

Felitti, Vincent J., Robert F. Anda, Dale Nordenberg, et al, "Relationship of Childhood Abuse and Household Dysfunction to Many of the Leading Causes of Death in Adults: The Adverse Childhood Experiences (ACE) Study," *American Journal of Preventive Medicine*, 14, no. 4 (1998): 245-258. www.acestudy.org/download.

Gibbs, Alfred P. *A Dreamer and His Wonderful Dream: or The Story of John Bunyan and "The Pilgrim's Progress"*. Fort Dodge: Walterick Printing Company.

Harris, R. Laird, Gleason L. Archer, Bruce K. Waltke, eds. *Theological Wordbook of the Old Testament,* Vol. I. Chicago: Moody Press, 1981.

Keller, W. Phillip. *Wonder O' the Wind.* London: Hodder & Stoughton Ltd, 1984.

Lewis, C.S. *A Grief Observed*; quoted in Philip Yancey, *Where Is God When It Hurts?* Grand Rapids: Zondervan, 1990.

Lewis, C.S. *The Complete C.S. Lewis Signature Classics.* San Francisco: HarperCollins, 2002.

MacDonald, Gordon. *The Life God Blesses.* Nashville: Thomas Nelson Inc., 1994.

McGrath, Alister E. *Suffering and God.* Grand Rapids: Zondervan Publishing House, 1995.

Mitchell, Connie. "Treasures of darkness", *Servant* 81, September 22, 2009, 12-14.

Norwood, Robin. *Why Me. Why This. Why Now: A Guide to Answering Life's Toughest Questions.* Toronto: McClelland & Stewart Inc., 1994.

Nouwen, Henri J. M. *The Inner Voice of Love: A Journey Through Anguish to Freedom.* New York: Image Books, 1998.

Packer, J.I. and Carolyn Nystrom. *Never Beyond Hope: How God Touches & Uses Imperfect People.* Downers Grove: InterVarsity Press, 2000.

Patterson, Ben. *Waiting: Finding Hope When God Seems Silent* Downers Grove: InterVarsity Press, 1989.

Piper, John. *When the Darkness Will Not Lift: Doing What We Can While We Wait for God—and Joy.* Wheaton: Crossway Books, 2006.

Piper, John. *Filling up the Afflictions of Christ: The Cost of Bringing the Gospel to the Nations in the Lives of William Tyndale, Adoniram Judson, and John Paton.* Wheaton: Crossway Books, 2009.

Pratney, Winkie. *The Thomas Factor.* Old Tappan: A Chosen Book, 1989.

Roper, David. *A Burden Shared.* Grand Rapids: Discovery House Publishers, 1991.

Roper, David. *The Strength of a Man: Encouragement for Today.* Grand Rapids: Discovery House Publishers, 1989.

Saint John of the Cross. *Dark Night of the Soul, 3rd ed.* Translated and edited by E. Allison Peers. Grand Rapids: Christian Classics Ethereal Library, n.d. www.ccel.org/ccel/john_cross/dark_night.i.html.

Schaeffer, Edith. *Affliction.* Old Tappan: Fleming H. Revell Company, 1978.

Schuller, Robert H. *Turning Hurts into Halos and Scars into Stars.* Nashville: Thomas Nelson Inc., 1999.

Sherman, Dean. *Spiritual Warfare: For Every Christian*. Seattle: YWAM Publishing, 1990.

Swindoll, Charles R. *Encourage Me: Caring Words for Heavy Hearts*. Grand Rapids: Zondervan Publishing House, 1993.

Tada, Joni Eareckson and Steve Estes. *When God Weeps: Why Our Sufferings Matter to the Almighty*. Grand Rapids: Zondervan Publishing House, 1997.

Thomas, Gary L. Seeking the Face of God. Eugene: Harvest House Publishers, 1994.

Trebesch, Shelley G. *Isolation: A Place of Transformation in the Life of a Leader*. Altadena: Barnabas Publishers, 1997.

Verwer, George. *Out of the Comfort Zone: Vision! Grace! Action!* Carlisle, England: OM Publishing, 2000.

Wiersbe, Warren *Why Us?: When Bad Things Happen to God's People*. Leicester, England: InterVarsity Press, 1984.

Wilson, Susan. *Hawkes Cove*. New York: Pocket Books, 2000.

Wright, Lorraine M. *Spirituality, Suffering, and Illness: Ideas for Healing*. Philadelphia: F. A. Davis Company, 2005.

Yancey, Philip. *Where Is God When It Hurts?* Grand Rapids: Zondervan, 1990.

CPSIA information can be obtained
at www.ICGtesting.com
Printed in the USA
FSOW04n0914230415
6662FS